# THE AI-DRIVEN PROCUREMENT PLAYBOOK

A Global Professional's Guide, Global Strategies, Prompts, and Case Studies for Intelligent Supply Chain Leaders

## DIAMOND FIANKA

**Disclaimer**

This book contains fictionalized and illustrative case studies, scenarios, and examples created solely for educational purposes. Any resemblance to actual companies, organizations, individuals, or events living or dead is purely coincidental.

The content is provided for general informational purposes only and does not constitute legal, financial, procurement, compliance, or professional advice. The author makes no representations or warranties regarding outcomes resulting from the application of ideas, tools, or technologies discussed and disclaims any liability arising from their use.

References to artificial intelligence, analytics, or related technologies are illustrative and non-endorsement in nature. Performance and outcomes may vary depending on data quality, governance, regulatory context, and human judgment.

This publication reflects the author's views at the time of writing and does not represent the views of any current or former employer.

For permissions, inquiries, or reproduction requests, please contact the author. theplatformint@gmail.com;diamond.fianka@gmail.com

Social Network: linkedin.com/in/diamondfianka

ISBN 978-1-0684623-3-7

First Edition: November 2025

## Dedication

To God the ultimate source of wisdom, clarity, and creative insight that made this work possible.

To my family, whose love, patience, and prayers have been the constant foundation beneath every new pursuit. Special appreciation to my wife, Mary Fianka, for the countless sacrifices and unwavering support.

To Mark, whose encouragement during our conversation at the inaugural CIPS Volunteer Conference and Awards in October 2025 transformed a simple idea into a written reality. Your belief in purposeful leadership continues to inspire.

To Bolutife, John, and Stephen, I sincerely thank you for your continued support and for taking the time to review the draft.

To every friend, colleague, and mentor who has contributed seen or unseen to this journey.

And to all procurement and supply chain leaders across the world who dare to innovate responsibly, shaping a future where intelligence and integrity walk hand in hand

## Acknowledgments

With gratitude to the procurement and supply chain community, whose curiosity, collaboration, and courage continue to redefine leadership in the digital era.

Special thanks to colleagues, mentors, and friends whose insights and encouragement supported this work.

## Preface AI-Driven Procurement: From Efficiency to Intelligence

Procurement has always been a balance between logic and judgment. Behind every purchase order lies a story of trust, timing, and trade-offs. Today, that story is being rewritten by artificial intelligence. Yet, contrary to popular fear, this new chapter is not about machines taking over decision making it is about professionals learning to think with machines.

### A New Era of Intelligent Partnership

Across industries and continents, procurement teams are facing a convergence of pressures: global supply volatility, cost inflation, carbon accountability, and social-value expectations. Traditional spreadsheets and supplier databases can no longer keep pace. Artificial intelligence, once a theoretical promise, is now the most practical ally for navigating this complexity.

AI does not remove human judgment; it multiplies its reach. Algorithms can digest thousands of data points in seconds, revealing patterns that even the most experienced category manager might overlook. But it is still the professional who must interpret the insight, weigh the ethical implications, and make the final call. This partnership between human discernment and digital precision defines the future of procurement.

### Why This Playbook Exists

The purpose of this playbook is simple: to help procurement and supply-chain professionals harness AI responsibly, confidently, and effectively. It offers global context, practical frameworks, and human centered guidance, helping readers move beyond experimentation toward enterprise-level adoption.

While the market is saturated with technical white papers and vendor case studies, very few resources speak directly to practitioners, those who manage contracts, negotiate with suppliers, and translate data into value every day. This book bridges that gap. It demystifies AI by focusing on use rather than hype.

## Three Shifts Shaping the Profession

### From process to prediction

Efficiency is no longer enough. Procurement leaders are judged by foresight the ability to anticipate risk and opportunity before competitors do. Predictive analytics and machine learning now make this possible.

### From transactions to transparency

Global supply chains operate under a new social contract. Stakeholders expect ethical sources, carbon accountability, and fair labour practices. AI enables visibility into multi-tier supplier networks, turning compliance into credibility.

### From automation to augmentation

The real promise of AI is not automation but augmentation. Machines handle volume and speed; humans provide judgment and empathy. Together they deliver decisions that are not only faster but fairer and more sustainable.

## The Trust Imperative

Every conversation about AI must also be a conversation about trust. Procurement data prices, supplier performance, and payment terms are among the most sensitive information any organisations hold. Understandably, professionals worry about data leakage or misuse. This playbook addresses those fears head-on, explaining how modern AI platforms protect privacy and how users can maintain control through settings that allow them to clear history, download data, or disable training.

Trust begins with understanding. When we know how a system works and where our choices sit within its technology becomes less intimidating and more empowering.

## Global Relevance

Procurement is both local and global. Whether you manage raw materials in Lagos, facilities in London, or logistics in Kuala Lumpur, the principles of ethical AI apply. The examples in this book draw from multiple regions to ensure inclusivity: African suppliers leveraging predictive risk analytics; European FMCG firms embedding AI in sustainability audits; Asian manufacturers using digital twins for supply-chain simulation. The challenges differ, but the aspiration is shared to deliver value without violating trust.

## How to Use This Book

Each chapter builds on the previous one, moving from understanding to application, from tools to transformation.

Chapters 1–3 outline the context and opportunity of AI in procurement.

Chapters 4–6 teach you how to collaborate with AI systems and craft powerful prompts.

Chapters 7–8 focus on governance, ethics, and building an AI-ready organisation.

Chapters 9–13 explore future trends, human trust, and practical readiness frameworks.

Each chapter ends with Key Takeaways and In-Practice Prompts so you can test ideas within your own environment.

**A Human Invitation**

Procurement has always been made for people who buy, those who supply, and those whose lives are touched by every transaction. AI, when used ethically, strengthens those connections by removing noise and revealing insight. The greatest asset in this transformation is not the algorithm but the professional who learns to guide it.

As you read this playbook, take what fits, question what doesn't, and adapt what inspires you. The goal is not perfection but progress: one ethical decision, one transparent contract, one responsible innovation at a time.

**"AI will not replace procurement; professionals who use AI wisely will."**

Welcome to the era of intelligent procurement where data serves people, and people serve purpose.

**- Diamond Fianka**

## About The Author

Diamond Fianka, FCIPS, is a dynamic educator, procurement strategist, and leadership mentor dedicated to advancing intelligent, ethical, and sustainable supply chains. A Fellow of the Chartered Institute of Procurement & Supply (CIPS), he brings over a decade of cross-sector experience in strategic sourcing, ESG integration, and AI enabled supply-chain transformation.

He holds a First Class BSc in Computer Science from Benson Idahosa University and an MSc in Logistics and Supply Chain Management from Sheffield Hallam University, graduating with distinction. His professional and academic work bridges technology, ethics, and human-centered leadership helping organisations move from efficiency to intelligence.

As the founder of ThePlatform, an online mentorship community, Diamond empowers emerging professionals through practical guidance, digital literacy, and purpose-driven leadership.

Born into the family of Chief Sibisaba Samson Fianka of the Yeye community, his heritage continues to shape his values of integrity, service, and excellence. Married to Mary Tolu Fianka and father to Tamaraakpo Sibisaba Fianka, he inspires others through faith, mentorship, and lifelong learning.


Books by the Author

• Rising Above: Turning Your Academic Struggles into Success

# Contents

# CHAPTER 1

## AI IN PROCUREMENT AND SUPPLY CHAIN

### Why AI Is a Game-Changer in Procurement

Procurement has always been a discipline built on judgment under pressure. Every sourcing decision balances cost, quality, risk, and time, often with imperfect information. In a typical week, professionals must evaluate suppliers, negotiate contracts, manage delivery performance, and track compliance all while responding to market volatility and internal demands for savings. For decades, experience and intuition were the differentiators. But the data age has changed the playing field.

The modern economy moves faster than any human spreadsheet can follow. Commodity prices shift overnight, geopolitical events ripple instantly through shipping routes, and ESG standards evolve by the quarter. Procurement teams are expected not only to manage these variables but to predict them. That is where **Artificial Intelligence (AI)** moves from concept to competitive necessity.

AI can process and pattern-match across massive data sets supplier performance metrics, market indices, weather forecasts, trade-flow data, and even social-media sentiment within seconds. Properly applied, this intelligence gives professionals something they have long craved: the ability to see around corners.

### From Data to Decisions

Traditionally, decision-making relied on static reports that showed what had happened. AI enables a shift to what is happening and what will happen next. A well-designed AI model can flag early warning signs of supplier distress, simulate alternative sourcing scenarios, and suggest mitigation strategies before problems escalate.

Imagine a global electronics manufacturer sourcing 200 Tier-2 suppliers across Asia. Previously, risk assessment involved multiple spreadsheets, email updates, and delayed financial checks. Today, an AI enabled system can create a live dashboard within hours, complete with financial health indicators, ESG alerts, and delivery performance scores. What once required days of manual analysis now appears in near real time allowing leaders to focus on strategy, not data gathering.

## The Evolution of Digital Tools in Supply Chain

The digital journey of procurement has unfolded in three major waves:

**ERP Automation (1990s–2000s)**: Enterprise Resource Planning systems standardised purchase orders and approvals, improving control but offering only backward-looking data.

**Business Intelligence (BI) and Dashboards (2010s)**: Visual analytics revealed spend trends and compliance gaps but still depended on manual interpretation.

**Artificial Intelligence & Machine Learning (2020s onward)**; Predictive and prescriptive tools now anticipate disruptions, optimise supplier choices, and even generate contract recommendations.

This third wave marks a **paradigm shift**: procurement professionals evolved from data reporters to strategic advisors.

They are no longer asking, **"What happened?"** but **"What will happen and what should we do about it?"**

Global Forces Driving AI Adoption

Several macro trends make AI indispensable:

**Complex Global Sourcing**: Supply networks span continents, requiring central visibility and predictive insight.

**Market Volatility**: Rapid shifts in raw material prices, freight costs, and exchange rates demand instant scenario planning.

**Sustainability & ESG Mandates**: Regulators and consumers expect evidence of ethical sourcing; AI automates data collection and reporting.

**Data Abundance**: Organisations possess terabytes of operational data that have remained under-analysed until now.

**Remote Work & Distributed Teams**: AI dashboards and automated workflows keep global teams aligned across time zones.

**Sample Mini Case Study 1**

**Predictive Savings at a European FMCG Company (Illustrative Case)**

*The following mini case is a fictional example designed to illustrate a common application of AI-driven analytics in supply-chain cost optimization. It does not describe a specific company or real-world engagement.*

A European fast-moving consumer-goods (FMCG) producer was experiencing sustained increases in freight costs across its Asian supply network. Leadership suspected structural inefficiencies but lacked granular visibility by lane, carrier, and transport mode.

Using AI-driven analytics, the supply-chain team analyzed historical freight data to identify cost anomalies and performance outliers across routes and providers. The system then simulated alternative multimodal routing scenarios, balancing cost, lead time, and service reliability.

The analysis indicated that selective route redesign and carrier reallocation could reduce freight spending without operational disruption. Implementing these recommendations resulted in an estimated 12% reduction in logistics costs, with no adverse impact on delivery times. Notably, the final board presentation was delivered entirely through live AI dashboards, enabling executives to explore scenarios dynamically rather than relying on static slides.

**Leadership Insight:**

AI creates the most value when it shifts leadership conversations from static reports to dynamic, decision-driven dialogue.

**From Automation to Augmentation**

There is a subtle but crucial distinction between automation and augmentation. Automation replaces repetitive tasks; augmentation enhances human capability. AI can categorise invoices, classify spending, or draft contract clauses but only humans can evaluate context, empathy, and ethics. When both work together, the outcome is more resilient decisions, faster negotiations, and deeper supplier relationships.

**Automation saves time; augmentation builds trust.**

## The Power of Prompting

AI's usefulness depends on how we communicate with it. Poorly phrased queries lead to generic results; structured prompts yield strategic insights. For instance:

**Vague:** "Analyse supplier risk."

**Precise:** "You are a global supply-chain risk consultant. Assess 120 Tier-2 suppliers in Asia for financial, operational, and ESG risk. Provide a scoring matrix and three mitigation actions suitable for executive review.

The second prompt transforms AI from a tool into a partner. Throughout this playbook, we will refine this craft of prompting until it becomes second nature.

## From Data Overload to Actionable Insight

Procurement has never lacked data; it has lacked clarity.

Invoices, supplier evaluations, shipment updates, audit reports, each system stores its own truths in different formats. When data lives in silos, professionals drown in information but starve for insight.

AI resolves this paradox by integrating, cleansing, and interpreting disparate datasets. Through natural-language queries or visual dashboards, a category manager can now ask, "Which suppliers contribute most to carbon emissions in our Tier-2 network?" and receive an answer in seconds complete with supporting evidence and recommended actions.

The key shift is psychological: instead of spending 80 percent of their time collecting and reconciling data, procurement teams can now devote that energy to **strategic execution.**

**Sample Mini Case Study 2**

**Proactive Risk Mitigation in Asia (Illustrative Case)**

*The following mini case is a fictional example designed to illustrate a common application of AI-driven analytics in procurement and supply-chain risk management. It does not describe a specific company or real-world engagement.*

A multinational electronics manufacturer depended heavily on suppliers in Southeast Asia for critical micro-components. In previous years, unexpected currency volatility and raw-material shortages had triggered production delays, exposing the organization to operational and financial risk.

To improve early risk detection, the procurement team trained an AI model on five years of supplier delivery performance, financial indicators, and external news-feed data. The system generated a live supplier risk heatmap, continuously updating risk scores based on emerging signals across geopolitical, financial, and operational dimensions.

The model identified five suppliers as high risk nearly two months before any material disruption occurred. This early warning enabled the company to renegotiate payment terms, activate alternate suppliers, and adjust inventory buffers. As a result, the organization avoided an estimated £2.8 million in production downtime costs while maintaining supply continuity.

**Leadership Insight:** Risk management becomes a competitive advantage when leaders act on weak signals before they become visible crises.

**Lesson:** Data predicts nothing without pattern recognition and pattern recognition scales only with AI.

## The Cultural Dimension of Digital Transformation

Technology succeeds or fails in culture. AI adoption is not a software rollout; it is a mindset shift. Teams must learn to trust algorithmic suggestions without surrendering judgment.

Strong leadership communicates that **AI is a co-pilot, not a threat**. When managers model curiosity asking, "What did the data show you?" instead of "Who made the mistake?" **they replace fear with learning.**

A helpful principle is the **3 Ts of AI Culture**:

**Transparency**: Explain how data is sourced, and decisions are generated.

**Training**: Upskill teams to read dashboards and question outputs.

**Trust**: Validate early successes publicly so confidence compounds.

## Sustainability and ESG as Strategic Catalysts

AI is accelerating a second revolution: the integration of **Environmental, Social and Governance (ESG)** priorities into everyday sourcing. Where manual audits once took months, AI can scan supplier disclosures, social-media sentiment, and certification databases in hours. The result is continuous compliance rather than annual check-ups.

A global apparel brand, for example, used AI to analyse 200 supplier sustainability reports. The model identified inconsistencies in energy-use data and recommended targeted audits. Within a year, the carbon intensity per garment fell by 18 per cent. Cost control and climate responsibility became the same conversation.

## Global Collaboration in Real Time

Modern supply chains rarely sleep. AI tools embedded in collaboration platforms (such as Copilot, Gemini for Workspace, or ChatGPT Enterprise) enable procurement teams in different time zones to share dashboards, translate supplier communications, and update risk alerts simultaneously. The outcome is a flatter, faster organisation one that learns as a single global brain. Technology equalises geography; collaboration humanises it.

## Ethics and Data Control: Keeping the Human in the Loop

No discussion of AI in procurement is complete without addressing the question every professional ask: "Is my data safe?". Leading enterprise AI providers now enforce strict **privacy-by-design** standards: User data is **encrypted in transit and at rest**. Corporate deployments can **disable model training for** internal prompts. Individual users can **delete chat histories** or **export data** at any time.

Similar controls exist across platforms: Google Gemini offers "no-retention mode"; Microsoft Copilot respects tenant boundaries within Microsoft 365; and Grammarly's business accounts guarantee zero model training from customer text.

The message is clear; **you remain in control.** Responsible adoption begins with knowing which settings protect confidentiality and training teams to use them as instinctively as they lock an office drawer.

**Sample Mini Case Study 3**

**Ethical Automation in Healthcare Procurement (Illustrative Case)**

*The following mini case is a fictional example designed to illustrate the responsible use of AI in healthcare procurement. It does not describe a specific organization or real-world deployment.*

A European hospital group introduced AI to automate supplier credential checks. Early pilots raised privacy concerns among clinicians. The procurement leader responded by establishing a "digital ethics board" that reviewed every data source before go-live. The system was launched with complete transparency: staff could see what data was collected, how it was used, and when it was deleted. Within 6 months, supplier approval time fell from 14 days to 3 days, with no privacy complaints.

**Leadership Insight:** Trust is not a constraint on automation; it is a prerequisite for scaling it. Transparency transforms fear into participation.

## The New Skill Set for Procurement Leaders

As automation handles routine tasks, leadership value migrates toward three human competencies:

**Interpretation**: translating AI output into strategic recommendations.

**Influence**: using data storytelling to secure stakeholder buy-in.

**Integrity:** ensuring every digital shortcut aligns with organisational ethics.

Tomorrow's category manager is part analyst, part communicator, and part guardian of digital trust.

## Sample Prompt

"You are a global procurement strategist. Summarise key AI trends affecting procurement and supply-chain management in 2025, including predictive analytics, generative AI, and ESG applications. For each trend, list one potential benefit and one implementation risk suitable for executive discussion."

## Key Takeaways

- AI elevates procurement from operational support to strategic leadership.
- Automation saves time; augmentation builds insight and trust.
- Predictive analytics and real-time dashboards convert data overload into foresight.
- Privacy and ethical control are non-negotiable foundations for adoption.

The most valuable skill is not coding—but **critical questioning**.

## CHAPTER 2

## CORE CHALLENGES IN PROCUREMENT AND SUPPLY CHAIN

### Every Profession Evolves Through Constraint.

Procurement is no different. The global supply ecosystem, once predictable, linear, and local, has become complex, dynamic, and often fragile. Even before the COVID-19 pandemic, procurement teams were managing cost pressure, compliance risk, and sustainability demands. Post-pandemic, those pressures multiplied: logistics bottlenecks, inflationary shocks, new ESG mandates, and the relentless expectation that procurement must "do more with less."

Artificial Intelligence offers powerful tools, but to use them effectively, leaders must first understand the terrain of the persistent challenges that technology must address rather than disguise.

### Complexity Of Global Sourcing

**The Modern Supply Web**

Gone are the days of a tidy supply chain. Today's network is a multidimensional web of Tier-1, Tier-2, and Tier-3 suppliers spread across continents. Each node interacts with multiple others; disruption in one corner can ripple globally within hours. Visibility becomes mission-critical, yet most Organisations still manage supplier data through static spreadsheets and isolated ERPs.

### Core Pain Points

**Geographical dispersion:** Different time zones, languages, and regulatory regimes.

**Opaque sub-tiers:** Limited sight of Tier-2 / Tier-3 suppliers.

**Cultural variance:** Diverse norms around communication, quality, and accountability.

**Information latency:** the delay between an event and awareness.

**Sample Case Study 4**

**Network Visibility in a European Automotive Supply Chain (Illustrative Case)**

*The following mini case is a fictional example designed to illustrate the use of AI-based supply-network mapping to identify hidden dependencies and structural risks. It does not describe a specific company or real-world engagement.*

A European automotive manufacturer sourced microchips from Asia and aluminum components from South America, operating through a multi-tier supplier network with limited visibility beyond Tier-1 partners. When a localized port strike caused shipment delays, the company discovered that a Tier-3 supplier supporting a critical component had no backup tooling, exposing an unexpected single point of failure.

To address this vulnerability, the procurement function deployed AI-based network-mapping capabilities to trace material flows across tiers and geographies. The analysis highlighted several hidden chokepoints and dependency clusters that had not been visible through traditional supplier reporting.

Within eight weeks, the company established dual-sourcing arrangements and contingency tooling plans for the most critical nodes in the network. These actions reduced estimated future production downtime risk by 20%, materially strengthening supply resilience without increasing baseline operating costs.

**Leadership Insight:** Resilience is built by illuminating what leaders cannot see; not by optimizing what they already know.

## AI Opportunity

AI systems can consolidate customs data, logistics feeds, and supplier-performance metrics into unified dashboards. Machine-learning models detect anomalies such as rising lead times or abnormal order cancellations, giving leaders early warning of bottlenecks.

## Supplier Risk and Performance Management

## Risk Multipliers

Procurement professionals face five intertwined risk types:

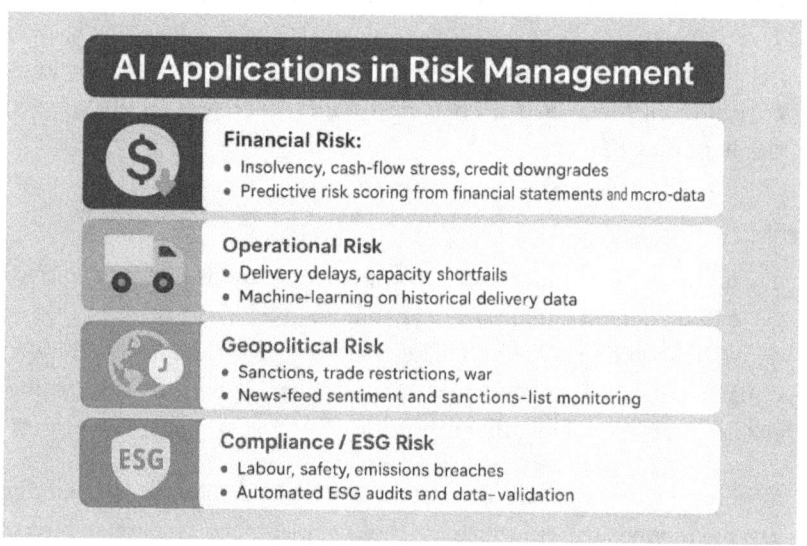

**Sample Mini Case Study 5**

**Supplier Early Warning System (Illustrative Case)**

*The following mini case is a fictional example designed to illustrate the use of AI-driven early warning systems in supplier risk monitoring. It does not describe a specific company or real-world deployment.*

A global electronics manufacturer sought to strengthen supply continuity by improving its ability to detect early signs of supplier financial distress. Traditional monitoring relied on periodic reviews and lagging indicators, often identifying issues only after disruptions had already begun.

To address this gap, the procurement team implemented an early AI-driven warning system that combined internal shipment performance logs with third-party supplier credit data. The model continuously assessed payment behavior, delivery reliability, and financial health to identify emerging risk patterns.

The system flagged two strategic suppliers exhibiting deteriorating payment cycles well before contractual breaches occurred. This early insight enabled procurement to renegotiate commercial terms, qualify alternate suppliers, and adjust sourcing plans proactively. As a result, the organization avoided potential production losses while maintaining stable supplier relationships.

**Leadership Insight:** The value of AI in risk management lies not in prediction accuracy alone, but in the time it gives leaders to act.

Cost Pressures and Market Volatility
**The Inflation Whiplash**

Commodity swings, freight surcharges, and currency fluctuations erode margins faster than traditional quarterly reviews can respond. Procurement must transform from price-taker to price-predictor.

## How AI Helps

**Dynamic Forecasting:** Predicts raw-material cost trends using economic indicators.

**Scenario Simulation:** Tests impact of different sourcing strategies or currencies.

**Contract Re-Indexation:** Generates clause recommendations to share volatility risk.

## Sustainability and ESG Compliance

**From Policy to Practice**

Sustainability has shifted from corporate aspiration to regulatory expectation. Procurement sits at the epicenter, responsible for Scope 3 emissions, supplier labour standards, and ethical governance.

**Challenges**

- Inconsistent ESG data formats.
- Manual supplier surveys with low response rates.
- Difficulty verifying real-world performance beyond self-reports.

## AI Solutions

AI platforms extract, normalise, and score ESG data from sustainability reports, satellite imagery, and IoT sensors—natural-language processing flags potential non-compliance in supplier disclosures.

**Sample Mini Case Study 6**

**AI-Enabled Sustainability Auditing in a Global FMCG Network (Illustrative Case)**

*The following mini case is a fictional example designed to illustrate the use of AI-driven analytics in sustainability monitoring and ESG assurance. It does not describe a specific company or real-world implementation.*

A multinational fast-moving consumer goods (FMCG) company sought to improve the accuracy and credibility of its sustainability reporting across a global supplier base. Manual reviews of supplier disclosures were time-consuming and offered limited ability to detect inconsistencies on a scale.

To strengthen oversight, the organization deployed an AI model to analyze sustainability disclosures from 150 suppliers, focusing on reported water-usage patterns and variance across comparable facilities and regions. The system flagged anomalies and outliers that warranted closer examination, enabling the company to prioritize on-site and third-party audits more effectively.

Targeted follow-up audits revealed opportunities for operational improvements and more accurate reporting. Within one year, the company reduced total water consumption by 12% and strengthened transparency across its supply network, contributing to improved investor confidence and ESG ratings.

**Leadership Insight:** Credible sustainability performance depends on leaders' ability to distinguish real progress from well-intentioned reporting.

Decision-Making Under Uncertainty
**The Pressure Cooker**

Procurement leaders often decide with incomplete data and intense time constraints. Market shocks, pandemics, strikes, cyber-attacks demand rapid choices where perfect information is impossible.

AI offers probabilistic insight, not prophecy. It can run "what-if" simulations that illuminate trade-offs, allowing humans to choose with greater confidence.

**Sample Mini Case Study 7**

**AI-Guided Contingency Planning in Pharmaceutical Packaging (Illustrative Case)**

*The following mini case is a fictional example designed to illustrate the use of AI-enabled scenario modeling for supply-chain contingency planning in the pharmaceutical sector. It does not describe a specific company or real-world incident.*

A pharmaceutical manufacturer faced the risk of production disruption when port congestion threatened the timely delivery of critical packaging materials used for regulated drug products. Given strict quality, safety, and compliance requirements, traditional rerouting decisions carried significant operational and regulatory risk.

To support rapid decision-making, the company leveraged an AI-enabled dashboard capable of modeling multiple contingency logistics scenarios in real time. The system evaluated three alternative routing options, comparing them across cost, delivery reliability, regulatory constraints, and ESG compliance factors.

Using these insights, executives selected the option that best balanced financial impact, supply continuity, and sustainability objectives. The decision was implemented swiftly, allowing the organization to avoid production delays while maintaining compliance with pharmaceutical quality and governance standards.

**Leadership Insight:** In high-stakes environments, AI's greatest contribution is not speed alone, but structured clarity under pressure.

## Global Regulatory and Compliance Challenges

Different regions impose distinct rules: EU CSRD reporting, U.S. Dodd-Frank Act, U.K. Modern Slavery Act, African local-content policies, and Asia-Pacific data-protection laws. Without automation, tracking compliance across jurisdictions overwhelms teams.

AI can:

- Parse contract text for missing legal clauses.
- Monitor supplier locations against sanctions lists.
- Generate ready-ready compliance reports.

## Visibility and Transparency
### End to End Insight

Accurate supply chain visibility means knowing not just who your suppliers are but how they operate. Yet data silos across ERP, SRM, logistics, and finance make this nearly impossible manually. AI-powered control towers integrate these feeds, offering predictive alerts and 360-degree transparency.

**Sample Case Study 8**

**End-to-End Visibility in a Global Apparel Supply Network (Illustrative Case)**

*The following mini case is a fictional example designed to illustrate the use of AI-enabled end-to-end visibility for proactive disruption management in the apparel industry. It does not describe a specific company or real-world event.*

A global fashion brand sought to improve coordination across a complex supply network spanning raw-material suppliers, manufacturing partners, distribution centers, and retail markets. Limited visibility beyond Tier-1 suppliers had previously constrained the company's ability to respond quickly to upstream disruptions.

To address this, the organization unified supplier production schedules, warehouse inventory data, and international shipping information into a single AI-enabled visibility platform. The system continuously monitored upstream signals and dependency patterns across tiers.

When a Tier-2 supplier showed elevated risk of cotton shortages, the platform triggered early alerts, allowing procurement and logistics teams to reroute sourcing and adjust production plans of impact. These actions enabled the brand to avoid stockouts across European markets while maintaining seasonal delivery commitments.

**Leadership Insight:** Visibility only becomes strategic when it gives leaders time to intervene before customers feel the impact.

### Cultural and Change-Management Barriers

Technology adoption fails when people fear replacement. Procurement teams worry that AI will deskill their roles or expose errors. Leaders must reframe AI as assistance, not automation.

## Change Levers

**Involve Early:** Include practitioners in pilot design.

**Educate:** Offer prompt-crafting and ethics training.

**Celebrate Quick Wins:** Publicise measurable results.

Building trust converts skepticism into stewardship.

## Sample Prompt for Chapter 2

"You are a procurement risk-management consultant. Identify the top five global challenges facing supply-chain leaders in 2025 and outline one AI-based strategy to mitigate each. Provide a short example from an international context."

## Key Takeaways

- Global supply networks demand predictive visibility, not reactive firefighting.
- AI strengthens supplier-risk management through data fusion and early-warning analytics.
- Cost volatility and ESG pressures make proactive modelling essential.
- Compliance is now continuous; automation ensures consistency.
- The most significant barrier is cultural; success depends on trust and training.
- AI doesn't eliminate complexity; it illuminates it.
- With insight comes choice, and with choice comes control.

## CHAPTER 3

## AI APPLICATIONS ACROSS THE SUPPLY CHAIN

Artificial Intelligence is no longer an experiment reserved for data scientists; it is now a practical ally for procurement and supply-chain teams. Across industries, AI is transforming how professionals **analyse spending, predict risk, negotiate contracts, manage logistics, and report on sustainability**. The common thread is speed, foresight, and precision.

This chapter explores the main operational applications of AI, illustrated through real-world mini case studies and accompanied by sample prompts you can adapt for your own organisation.

### Spend Analysis and Cost Optimisation

### The Traditional Challenge

Manual spend analysis depends on inconsistent coding and delayed reporting. Different business units may use varying supplier names, currencies, or categories, leaving managers to reconcile chaos before making decisions.

### How AI Changes the Game

AI automatically:

- Classifies spend across thousands of suppliers and cost centers.
- Detects anomalies, duplicate payments, and pricing deviations.
- Generates visual dashboards that pinpoint cost-saving opportunities.

**Sample Mini Case Study 9**

**AI-Led Spend Transparency in a Global FMCG Organization (Illustrative Case)**

*The following mini case is a fictional example designed to illustrate the use of AI-driven analytics for spend transparency and procurement transformation. It does not describe a specific company or real-world engagement.*

A global consumer-goods company managing approximately $500 million in annual third-party spend struggled with fragmented supplier data and inconsistent transaction categorization. While total spend was visible at an aggregate level, leadership lacked clarity on duplication, leakage, and structural inefficiencies across categories and suppliers.

To address this, the organization deployed an AI-enabled spend analytics platform to cleanse supplier master data, normalize transaction records, and cluster spend by category and vendor. The system revealed patterns that had previously been obscured by inconsistent naming conventions and misclassified invoices.

The analysis identified approximately $12 million in duplicate or mis-categorized invoices and highlighted opportunities for supplier consolidation and improved category governance. These insights provided a clear foundation for corrective action and strategic sourcing decisions.

**Leadership Insight:** Transformation begins when leaders replace aggregate visibility with analytical truth.

**Sample Prompt**

"You are a procurement analyst. Review of $500 million global data. Identify top ten cost-reduction opportunities by category and region. Present recommendations in an executive-summary table."

Supplier Risk Assessment and Performance Management

AI brings continuous monitoring to supplier management.

## Capabilities

- Scrape open-source and subscription data for financial, operational, and ESG indicators.
- Scores suppliers using weighted models.
- Triggers alerts when risk thresholds rise.

**Sample Mini Case Study 10**

**Multi-Tier Risk Intelligence in an Asian Electronics Supply Network (Illustrative Case)**

*The following mini case is a fictional example designed to illustrate the use of AI-enabled multi-tier risk intelligence in complex electronics supply networks. It does not describe a specific company or real-world assessment.*

An electronics manufacturer sought to improve risk visibility across its extended supplier base, particularly at the Tier-2 level, where disruptions had historically been difficult to detect early. The company conducted a structured assessment covering 150 Tier-2 suppliers across Asia, spanning multiple component categories.

Using AI-driven analytics, the organization integrated shipment reliability metrics, supplier audit results, and third-party credit data into a continuously updated risk dashboard. The system dynamically scored suppliers based on emerging operational, financial, and compliance signals.

The analysis identified seven suppliers with elevated disruption risk well ahead of any visible failure. This early insight enabled procurement to negotiate alternative production capacity and adjust sourcing plans proactively. As a result, the company reduced estimated potential disruption losses by 20% while maintaining supply continuity.

**Leadership Insight:** Risk intelligence becomes strategic only when it reaches beyond Tier-1 visibility and into the hidden layers of the network.

### Sample Prompt

"You are a global supply-chain risk consultant. Evaluate 150 suppliers for financial, operational, and ESG risk. Produce a traffic-light matrix with recommended mitigation actions."

### Contract Analytics and Document Automation

Contracts anchor value but often hide obligations and risk in dense text.

AI text-analysis tools now act as tireless paralegals.

### Applications

- Extract key terms (expiry, payment, liability).
- Flag missing or inconsistent clauses.
- Generate compliant templates automatically.
- Track milestone reminders through workflow bots.

### Sample Mini Case Study 11

### AI-Accelerated Contract Intelligence in Global Logistics (Illustrative Case)

*The following mini case is a fictional example designed to illustrate the use of AI-enabled contract intelligence for legal and procurement efficiency. It does not describe a specific organization or real-world deployment.*

A global logistics company faced growing pressure to review and renew a large portfolio of supplier contracts, with more than 500 active agreements requiring legal and procurement scrutiny. Manual review processes were time-consuming, resource-intensive, and often delayed commercial negotiations.

To improve efficiency without compromising legal rigor, the organization deployed an AI-based contract intelligence solution to analyze contractual language at scale. The system automatically identified key clauses, flagged deviations from standard terms, and highlighted contracts missing required ESG and compliance provisions.

As a result, average contract review time was reduced by 60%, while legal teams gained greater consistency and transparency across renewals. Standardized contract templates were introduced to streamline future negotiations. Reflecting on the outcome, the legal team described the approach as "speed without shortcuts."

**Leadership Insight:** AI delivers leverage when it amplifies professional judgment rather than attempting to replace it.

**Sample Prompt**

"You are a procurement legal analyst. Review 50 supplier contracts. Identify missing performance or ESG clauses and summarise findings in a report suitable for executive review."

## Forecasting and Demand Planning

Accurate forecasting prevents both stockouts and excess inventory.

## AI Advantages

- Combines historical sales, seasonality, marketing calendars, and external signals (weather, macro-economic).
- Continuously learns from new data.
- Suggests optimal inventory buffers by region.

### Sample Mini Case Study 12

### AI-Augmented Demand Forecasting in a European Apparel Brand (Illustrative Case)

*The following mini case is a fictional example designed to illustrate the use of AI-enabled demand forecasting to support merchandising and inventory decisions in the apparel industry. It does not describe a specific company or real-world deployment.*

A European apparel brand faced recurring challenges with seasonal demand volatility, leading to overstock in some markets and stockouts in others. Traditional forecasting methods struggled to account for rapidly shifting consumer preferences, weather patterns, and promotional effects.

To improve planning accuracy, the company introduced an AI-based forecasting system that combined historical sales data, regional trends, promotional calendars, and external demand signals. Rather than replacing human planners, the system provided probabilistic forecasts and scenario ranges to support decision-making.

Within a single season, the brand reduced seasonal overstock by 15%, improved allocation accuracy across stores and regions, and lowered markdown-related margin losses. Planners reported higher confidence in decisions, noting that the system clarified trade-offs rather than prescribing outcomes. As one planner observed:

**Leadership Insight:** The strongest AI systems do not compete with human judgment; they make it measurable.

## Sample Prompt

"You are a demand-planning analyst. Forecast for next-quarter inventory of seasonal products across Europe. Highlight risk of overstock or stockout by market."

## Logistics Optimisation and Route Planning

Transportation is often procurement's largest controllable cost.

## AI Capabilities

- Real-time route Optimisation using traffic, weather, and port-congestion data.
- Predictive maintenance scheduling for fleet assets.
- Dynamic carrier selection for cost and emissions balance.

## Sample Mini Case Study 13

## AI-Optimized Last-Mile Network Design in African E-Commerce (Illustrative Case)

*The following mini case is a fictional example designed to illustrate the use of AI-driven network optimization for last-mile delivery in emerging e-commerce markets. It does not describe a specific company or real-world expansion.*

An e-commerce company expanding across multiple African markets faced rising last-mile delivery costs and inconsistent service levels. Rapid growth had outpaced the company's original warehouse locations, leading to longer delivery routes and uneven coverage across urban and peri-urban areas.

To address these challenges, the company deployed AI-based network optimization tools that analyzed delivery density, order frequency, road quality, and travel-time variability. The model simulated alternative warehouse placement and routing scenarios to balance speed, coverage, and operating cost.

Based on these insights, the organization relocated two fulfillment centers to better align with demand patterns. As a result, average delivery times were reduced by 18%, while last-mile operating costs fell by 12%, enabling profitable growth without sacrificing service reliability.

**Leadership Insight:** Growth becomes sustainable when network design is guided by data, not legacy assumptions.

**Sample Prompt**

"You are a logistics Optimisation consultant. Recommend strategies to cut transportation lead times 15 % for a regional African distribution network, considering warehouse placement and multi-modal transport."

## Sustainability and ESG Reporting
**The New Reporting Reality**

Stakeholders now demand traceable, auditable sustainability data. AI simplifies the collection and verification of ESG metrics.

**What It Does**

- Aggregates supplier carbon, labour, and governance data.
- Calculates Scope 1–3 emissions automatically.

- Suppliers and recommend improvement plans.

## Sample Mini Case Study 14

## AI-Driven ESG Transformation in a Global FMCG Supply Network (Illustrative Case)

*The following mini case is a fictional example designed to illustrate the use of AI-enabled sustainability analytics to drive emissions reduction across global supply chains. It does not describe a specific company or real-world ESG program.*

A global fast-moving consumer goods (FMCG) company sought to accelerate progress toward its emissions-reduction targets by improving visibility into supplier-level carbon performance. With sustainability data dispersed across regions and reporting standards, leadership lacked a reliable basis for prioritizing interventions.

To address this, the company deployed AI-driven analytics to collect and normalize sustainability data from 200 suppliers worldwide. The system calculated end-to-end carbon footprints across key categories and identified suppliers where renewable energy transitions would yield the greatest emissions impact.

Guided by these insights, the organization prioritized targeted supplier engagement, co-investment programs, and transition roadmaps. Over a three-year period, these actions contributed to an estimated 20% reduction in supply-chain-related emissions, strengthening both environmental performance and ESG credibility.

**Leadership Insight:** Meaningful ESG progress occurs when analytics guide where leaders focus effort—not just how they report outcomes.

**Sample Prompt**

"You are a sustainability consultant. Create an ESG assessment framework for 200 suppliers. Include scoring criteria for carbon, labour, and governance performance."

Supplier Collaboration and Innovation
AI enables shared visibility and predictive alignment between buyers and suppliers.

**Use Cases**

Collaborative forecasting and capacity planning.

Joint product development informed by data.

Automated performance feedback loops.

**Sample Mini Case Study 15**

**AI-Enabled Co-Innovation in Electronics Supply Partnerships (Illustrative Case)**

*The following mini case is a fictional example designed to illustrate how shared AI-driven insights can enable collaborative planning and co-innovation between manufacturers and strategic suppliers. It does not describe a specific company or real-world partnership.*

An electronics manufacturer sought to improve responsiveness and quality across a critical component supply base. Historically, demand forecasts were shared selectively, limiting suppliers' ability to plan capacity and optimize production schedules.

To address this, the manufacturer began sharing AI-generated demand forecasts with selected strategic suppliers through a shared planning platform. Both parties had visibility into the same demand assumptions, scenario ranges, and planning horizons, creating a common data foundation for joint decision-making.

Using these shared insights, manufacturers and suppliers collaboratively adjusted production schedules, optimized batch sizes, and aligned capacity investments. As a result, component lead times were reduced by 10%, yield quality improved, and planning volatility decreased. Trust between partners strengthened as both sides operated from a single, transparent data reality.

**Leadership Insight:** Collaboration accelerates when partners trust the data as much as they trust each other.

### Sample Prompt

"You are a procurement innovation consultant. Propose collaboration strategies with suppliers to reduce lead times and improve quality using predictive analytics."

### Real-Time Monitoring and Predictive Alerts

AI dashboards act as a digital control tower for the modern enterprise.

### Functions

- Track inventory, shipments, and supplier KPIs in real time.
- Send predictive alerts for potential disruptions.
- Enable proactive mitigation rather than reactive firefighting.

**Sample Mini Case Study 16**

**AI-Enabled Supply Continuity Monitoring in Pharmaceuticals (Illustrative Case)**

*The following mini case is a fictional example designed to illustrate the use of AI-driven real-time monitoring to safeguard production continuity in the pharmaceutical sector. It does not describe a specific company or real-world deployment.*

A pharmaceutical manufacturer sought to strengthen supply continuity for critical raw materials used in regulated drug production. Traditional monitoring relied on periodic status updates, often detecting risks only after supply disruptions had begun to materialize.

To improve early detection, the company deployed an AI-enabled continuity dashboard that analyzed real-time shipping data, transit delays, and upstream logistics signals. The system generated automated alerts when patterns indicated elevated risk of raw-material shortages.

By identifying potential disruptions two weeks earlier than previous processes, the organization was able to reroute orders, activate contingency suppliers, and adjust production sequencing. These actions enabled the company to maintain uninterrupted manufacturing operations despite external supply volatility.

**Leadership Insight:** Continuity is protected when leaders gain time to respond before disruption becomes visible.

## Sample Prompt

"You are a supply-chain analyst. Generate a live monitoring report combining supplier lead times, inventory levels, and logistics status. Highlight disruption risks and mitigation recommendations."

### AI for Procurement Governance and Audit

Governance ensures that efficiency never compromises ethics.

## Applications

Continuous audit of purchase orders for policy breaches.

Fraud detection through anomaly recognition.

Automated compliance documentation for regulators.

### Sample Mini Case Study 17

## AI-Enabled Integrity Auditing in the Public Sector (Illustrative Case)

*The following mini case is a fictional example designed to illustrate the use of AI-driven analytics to strengthen transparency, integrity, and compliance in public-sector procurement. It does not describe a specific agency or real-world audit.*

A government agency in Africa faced challenges monitoring procurement integrity across a large volume of public tenders. Manual review processes were resource-intensive and limited the agency's ability to detect subtle pricing anomalies or collusive behavior at scale.

To enhance oversight, the agency deployed AI-enabled analytics to review thousands of tender submissions. The system analyzed bid pricing patterns, vendor relationships, and historical award data to identify irregularities and risk indicators that warranted further investigation.

The AI-driven review flagged multiple cases of suspicious pricing behavior, enabling auditors to prioritize follow-up actions more effectively. As a result, the agency improved procurement compliance outcomes by an estimated 25%, strengthening transparency and public trust.

**Leadership Insight:** Integrity systems scale only when oversight evolves from manual inspection to analytical insight.

## Sample Prompt

"You are a procurement governance auditor. Review tender data for anomalies suggesting potential collusion or overpricing. Summarise findings for compliance reporting."

### Challenges and Watch-Points

While these applications show immense promise, leaders must manage several risks:

**Data Quality:** Garbage in, garbage out. Invest in cleansing and master-data management.

**Integration:** Ensure AI tools connect with ERP and SRM systems.

**Change Management:** Upskill teams and clarify roles for human oversight.

**Ethics:** Monitor for bias, especially in supplier scoring.

**Security:** Restrict access and use enterprise-grade encryption. Adoption succeeds when technology, process, and people mature together.

**Key Takeaways**

- AI applies across every procurement stage from spend visibility to ESG impact.
- Predictive analytics converts lagging indicators into leading decisions.
- Real-time dashboards replace static reporting with living intelligence.
- Governance and human oversight remain non-negotiable.
- Collaboration, not competition, defines the AI-empowered supply chain.
- Machines may see faster, but humans still see meaning. Together, they form the intelligent enterprise of tomorrow.

## CHAPTER 4

## HUMAN + AI COLLABORATION FRAMEWORK

Artificial intelligence can compute, correlate, and predict, but it cannot care. Procurement success, however, has always depended on care; care for ethics, relationships, and consequences. The future therefore belongs not to AI alone but to professionals who know how to **collaborate** with it. This chapter introduces a practical framework for that collaboration: how humans and machines divide labour, validate insights, and build mutual trust in a digital procurement environment.

### Why Collaboration, Not Replacement

Automation once threatened to erase roles; augmentation now expands them. Where algorithms process scale, humans interpret nuance.

**AI answers what and when; people decide why and whether.**

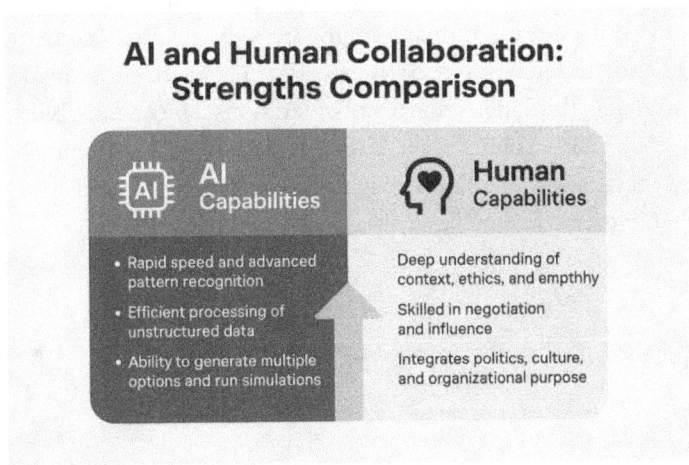

**"AI delivers information; humans deliver wisdom."**

The Collaboration Framework
## Step 1 – Define the Decision Loop

Each procurement decision passes through four stages:

- **Data Capture**: AI gathers and cleans inputs.
- **Insight Generation**: AI highlights anomalies or opportunities.
- **Interpretation**: Humans review, question, and adjust assumptions.
- **Action & Learning**: Humans decide; feedback is fed back into the model.

Embedding this loop in workflow systems ensures continual improvement rather than one-off analysis.

## Step 2: Clarify Roles

AI and humans need to work together because each brings strengths the other lacks. AI can process vast amounts of data quickly and spot patterns humans might miss, but it lacks context, judgment, and understanding of nuanced consequences. Humans provide strategic thinking, ethical considerations, and adaptability; ensuring that AI insights are applied wisely and effectively. Together, they create decisions that are faster, smarter, and more reliable than either could achieve alone.

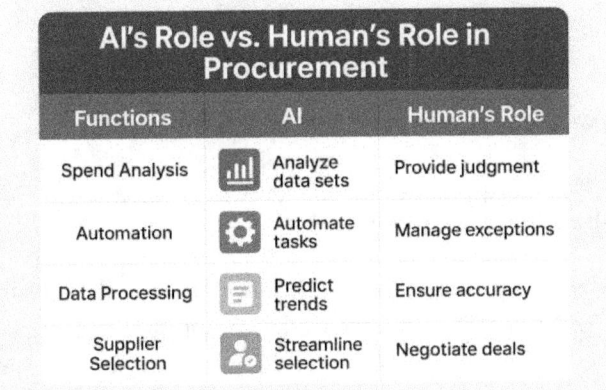

| Functions | AI | Human's Role |
|---|---|---|
| Spend Analysis | Analyze data sets | Provide judgment |
| Automation | Automate tasks | Manage exceptions |
| Data Processing | Predict trends | Ensure accuracy |
| Supplier Selection | Streamline selection | Negotiate deals |

## Step 3: Create the "Human-in-the-Loop" Control

The human-in-the-loop (HITL) principle means **that no AI decision is executed without human validation** when financial, ethical, or reputational stakes are high. It combines confidence with accountability — algorithms propose, professionals approve.

Practical methods:

- Approval checkpoints in automated workflows.
- Dual validation for supplier blacklisting.
- Ethics reviews for AI-generated contract clauses.

## Step 4: Build Trust through Transparency

Teams trust what they understand. AI systems should provide **explainability**, clear reasoning behind recommendations.

- Choose platforms that show:
- Data sources used.

- Weightings in risk or score models.
- Confidence levels for each prediction.

*When people see how AI thinks, they collaborate rather than compete.*

## Embedding Collaboration in Daily Workflow
**Example: Global Pharma Procurement**

A pharmaceutical group integrated AI dashboards into daily team huddles. Each morning, buyers reviewed live supplier-risk alerts; each Friday, they discussed which alerts AI mis-classified. Within six months:

- Risk-detection accuracy rose 18 %.
- Staff satisfaction scores increased 22 %.
- "AI fatigue" complaints disappeared.

The secret wasn't software; it was **ritual**: a shared rhythm of humans and data learning together.

## Overcoming Collaboration Barriers
Successful AI-human collaboration requires overcoming common barriers. Fear of job loss, data distrust, overreliance, skill gaps, and siloed teams can all block progress. By addressing these issues reframing AI as a skill amplifier, improving transparency, introducing checks, training staff, and fostering cross-functional squad organizations can unlock the full potential of AI and human partnerships.

## Overcoming AI Adoption Barriers

| Barrier | Root Cause | How to Respond |
|---|---|---|
| Fear of Job Loss | Unclear communication | Reframe AI as skill amplifier |
| Data Distrust | Lack of transparency | Educate on data sources & quality |
| Skill Gaps | "Black-box" comfort | Introduce manual spot-checks |
| Silo Culture | Limited digital literacy | Run prompt-engineering training |

Leadership must signal that using AI is a sign of expertise, not insecurity.

## Ethical and Privacy Dimensions

Ethics is the bridge between automation and acceptance. Procurement must guarantee that AI never compromises confidentiality or fairness.

**Practical safeguards**

- Use enterprise versions (ChatGPT Enterprise, Gemini for Workspace, Copilot for 365, Grammarly Business) with no data used for model training.
- Activate features that allow users to delete or export personal data.
- Maintain audit logs of AI-assisted decisions.

Transparency in these controls reduces resistance and anchors digital trust.

**Sample Mini Case Study 18**

## Human-in-the-Loop Decision-Making in Electronics Supply Management (Illustrative Case)

*The following mini case is a fictional example designed to illustrate the importance of human judgment in AI-assisted procurement decisions. It does not describe a specific company or real-world incident.*

A European electronics manufacturer used AI-driven monitoring to assess supplier delivery performance across its global supply base. The system flagged one long-standing Asian supplier as a chronic late-delivery risk and recommended immediate contract termination based on recent performance trends.

Before acting on the recommendation, procurement leaders conducted a human review of contextual factors. They identified that a regional port closure outside the supplier's control had caused the recent delays, while historical data showed a strong twelve-year partnership with consistent performance.

Rather than terminating the relationship, the company negotiated short-term logistics support and temporary routing adjustments to address the disruption. This approach preserved the supplier partnership, avoided contractual penalties, and stabilized deliveries without long-term damage to supply continuity.

**Leadership Insight:** The strongest AI decisions emerge when algorithms inform judgment not when they replace it. **AI recognised the pattern; humans recognised the context.**

### Building Collaborative Culture

### The 4 Cs of Digital Culture
**Curiosity**: Question outputs, explore alternatives.

**Competence**: Invest in continuous learning.

**Courage**: Adopt before it's perfect.

**Conscience**: Keep ethics central.

Managers should reward responsible experimentation; success is shared learning, not flawless prediction.

### Sample Prompt

"You are a procurement process consultant. Design a workflow that integrates AI insights into daily sourcing decisions for a multinational organization. Specify where human validation occurs and how data privacy is maintained."

### Key Takeaways

- The future is **Human + AI**, not Human vs AI.
- Define clear decision loops and validation checkpoints.
- Transparency creates trust, secrecy breeds resistance.
- Ethical governance protects both data and reputation.
- Collaboration culture turns technology into talent.
- When algorithms serve insight and humans serve integrity, procurement becomes truly intelligent.

# CHAPTER 5

## PROMPTING POWER: THE ART AND SCIENCE

Artificial intelligence is only as powerful as the instructions it receives. In human conversation, clarity defines understanding; in AI conversation, clarity defines outcome. The skill of writing structured, context-aware prompts transform AI from a general assistant into a **strategic collaborator**.

Procurement professionals already know the importance of specification. A poorly written supplier brief results in the wrong materials; a vague AI prompt yields irrelevant output. Prompting is therefore not a technical skill—it is a **strategic communication skill**.

This chapter introduces practical frameworks and examples for crafting effective prompts across procurement, supply chain management, and sustainability functions.

### Why Prompting Matters

AI models interpret language literally but contextually. They follow the data you provide, the constraints you set, and the clarity of your instructions. Consider two professionals tasked with assessing supplier risk.

**Prompt A:** "Analyse supplier risk."

Output: A generic paragraph listing common risks.

**Prompt B:** "You are a global procurement risk consultant with 15 years of experience. Analyse 200 Tier-2 suppliers across Asia for financial, operational, and ESG risks. Produce a scoring matrix, highlight the ten highest-risk suppliers, and suggest mitigation strategies suitable for executive presentation."

Prompt B gives the AI a role, scope, and deliverable results in a structured, actionable report.

**Key lesson:** the more specific the prompt, the more strategic the insight.

## The Procurement Power Prompt Framework

Procurement mirrors prompting both rely on clarity, context, and measurable outcomes. To make prompt simple, use the **5-Part Procurement Power Prompt Framework**:

Table 4.1: 5-Part Procurement Power Prompt Framework

| Step | Description | Example |
|---|---|---|
| **1. Role Definition** | Tell AI who it is supposed to be. | "You are a category manager for logistics." |
| **2. Context** | Describe the scenario or data background. | "We manage 200 suppliers in Africa and Europe." |
| **3. Task** | Specify what you want done. | "Assess freight-cost volatility for Q2." |
| **4. Output Format** | Define the form of results. | "Provide a 3-column table of causes, impacts, and mitigations." |
| **5. Constraints / Priorities** | Add boundaries (budget, tone, timeframe). | "Focus on actions under £1M and align with ESG targets." |

Combine all five and you have a precise, professional-grade prompt.

## Full Example Using Framework

"You are a global procurement strategist. Our company sources from 150 Tier-2 suppliers in Asia for electronic components.

Evaluate each supplier's financial, operational, and ESG risk. Produce a risk-scoring table highlighting the top 10 high-risk suppliers and recommend mitigation actions under a £1M cost constraint."

The output will likely include a well-organized matrix, prioritised recommendations, and narrative summaries exactly what an executive needs.

### Step By Step Prompting Process

### Step 1: Start with Role & Objective

AI performs better when it assumes a persona; it "thinks" like an expert.

### Step 2: Give Context Early

Include data scale, geography, or timeline.

Example: "We source materials from 200 suppliers across Southeast Asia with £400M annual spend."

### Step 3; Define the Deliverable

Be clear on whether you want bullet points, a report, a dashboard outline, or a summary.

### Step 4: Add Constraints

Budgets, ESG limits, or policy boundaries guide practicality.

Example: "Recommendations must align with ISO 20400 sustainability principles."

## Step 5: Review and Iterate

The first answer is a draft, not a decision. Refine prompts based on gaps in the output.

## Prompt Refinement: The Iterative Cycle

**Initial Prompt:** "List potential risks for suppliers in Asia."

**AI Output:** A general list: logistics delays, tariffs, weather, etc.

## Refined Prompt

"You are a risk consultant. Identify the top five supplier risks specific to electronics manufacturing in Asia in 2025. Classify each as financial, operational, or ESG. Provide impact scores (1–5) and suggest mitigation actions."

**Improved Output:** Now the AI generates structured insight that can be converted into a presentation or dashboard.

Prompting is not a one-shot effort; it's a **conversation of refinement.**

Common Prompting Mistakes

Table 5: Common Prompting Mistakes

| Mistake | Consequence | Correction |
|---------|-------------|------------|
| Vague instruction | Generic responses | Add detail and constraints |
| Missing context | Irrelevant output | Include region, category, data size |
| No format specified | Overly long text | Request bullet points or tables |
| Ignoring constraints | Unrealistic suggestions | Include budgets or ESG priorities |
| Overloading in one prompt | Confused or inconsistent answers | Break into smaller, layered prompts |

**Tip:** Treat each prompt as a procurement brief concise, outcome-focused, and measurable.

## Table 6: Prompting for Different Procurement Functions

| Function | Prompt Example | Output |
|----------|----------------|--------|
| Category Strategy | "You are a category manager. Develop a 12-month strategy for packaging materials sourced from Europe and Asia, considering cost, supplier performance, and ESG compliance." | Strategic plan with cost and risk analysis |
| Supplier Risk Assessment | "Assess 150 suppliers in Asia for financial, operational, and ESG risk. Rank them and recommend mitigations." | Risk matrix |
| Logistics Optimisation | "Propose strategies to reduce delivery lead times by 15% across Africa using multimodal routes." | Transport cost–benefit report |
| Contract Analysis | "Review 20 supplier contracts. Highlight missing clauses related to ESG or performance penalties." | Clause-gap table |
| ESG Monitoring | "Create a sustainability scorecard for 100 suppliers, including emissions, labour, and governance KPIs." | ESG scorecard |

## Mini-Case – Learning the Prompting Language in Procurement (Illustrative Case)

*The following mini case is a fictional example designed to illustrate how prompt discipline influences the reliability of AI-assisted analytical work. It does not describe a specific company or real-world deployment.*

A procurement team within an energy company began experimenting with generative AI to support spend categorization and reporting. While early pilots showed promise, results varied significantly: analysts using similar prompts often received inconsistent outputs, leading to rework and reduced confidence in the tool.

To address this, the team introduced a standardized 5-Part Prompting Framework across the department. The framework defined clear expectations for context, task, constraints, data inputs, and output format, ensuring that AI interactions followed a consistent structure regardless of user.

Once adopted, prompt consistency improved dramatically. Rework related to categorization errors fell by 35%, and reporting quality became more predictable and comparable across analysts. More importantly, the team developed a shared "prompting language," enabling AI to function as a reliable analytical assistant rather than an unpredictable experiment.

**Leadership Insight:** AI reliability improves not when tools get smarter, but when organizations learn how to speak to them consistently. **Standardising prompts create consistency, just as standardising specifications improves sourcing.**

## Layered and Sequential Prompting

Complex procurement problems are rarely solved in one question. Layered prompting means breaking a large task into structured, consecutive prompts; each refining the output of the last.

**Example: Supplier Rationalisation**

**Prompt 1**

"List all suppliers providing maintenance services across EMEA and categorise them by spend volume."

**Prompt 2**

"From the suppliers above, identify which show duplicate service scopes or overlapping regions."

**Prompt 3**

"Recommend a rationalizations strategy that maintains service coverage while reducing supplier count by 20 %."

Each stage clarifies thinking, much as category managers move from data gathering to analysis to action. Layered prompting reduces noise and produces executive-ready deliverables.

## Role Playing Prompts

AI becomes more effective when you assign it to a professional persona.

This technique helps generate specialised, context-aware outputs.

Table 7: Role-Playing Prompts

| Role | Prompt Example | Expected Output |
|---|---|---|
| Procurement Negotiator | "You are a senior negotiator preparing for a supplier meeting about price escalation. Draft three conversation strategies balancing relationship and cost control." | Negotiation playbook |
| ESG Auditor | "You are an ESG auditor reviewing a garment supplier in Bangladesh. Summarise key labour-practice risks and corrective-action priorities." | Risk summary with action plan |
| Contract Lawyer | "You are a contract lawyer for a UK manufacturer. Review the draft agreement and identify termination, indemnity, and data-protection gaps." | Clause-by-clause commentary |
| Supply-Chain Planner | "You are a supply-chain planner. Suggest three inventory strategies for volatile raw-material demand." | Comparative strategy matrix |

**Insight:** Role playing focuses AI's reasoning within a discipline, producing sharper, jargon accurate results.

## Scenario Simulation and 'What-If Analysis

Procurement thrives on foresight. AI can generate multiple "what-if" scenarios to prepare teams for disruption.

### Prompt Example

"You are a supply-chain risk analyst. Simulate three sourcing scenarios for microchips under potential trade restrictions between the US and China. Compare cost, lead-time, and ESG implications."

AI will return comparative tables and narrative commentary essential for board discussions.

### In Practice: Global Tech Manufacturer

By modelling five trade scenarios, one manufacturer avoided single-source dependency and saved £9 million in contingency costs.

The insights were later codified into a playbook for future geopolitical disruptions.

**Iterative Feedback Loops:** Iteration transforms AI from a one-time assistant into a learning partner.

Each feedback cycle should answer the question: What worked? What lacked context? What must change?

**Practical Method**

- Request a draft output.
- Review for gaps or over generalizations.
- Feed corrections back into a follow-up prompt.
- Ask for an improved version incorporating the feedback.

Example:

"Revise the supplier-risk table to weight ESG compliance 40 %, cost 30 %, and delivery reliability 30 %."

Within three iterations, outputs typically reach professional-report quality.

**Prompt Libraries and Governance**

To scale prompting across teams, create a shared **Prompt Library**, a repository of proven instructions for recurring tasks.

**Structure**

**Category:** spend analysis, risk, contracts, ESG, logistics.

**Prompt Template:** the tested text.

**Owner:** person responsible for updates.

**Review Date:** scheduled refresh to reflect policy or market changes.

A governance mechanism ensures accuracy and compliance, much like version control for policies. This avoids "prompt drift," where inconsistent wording causes inconsistent results.

## Evaluating Prompt Quality

High-quality prompts demonstrate five characteristics:

**Clarity**: no ambiguity in task.

**Context**: relevant background provided.

**Constraint**: boundaries and scope defined.

**Creativity**: room for nuanced solutions.

**Checkability**: measurable outputs for validation.

Use a quick self-review checklist: Does this prompt sound like a procurement brief I'd sign off?

## Cross Functional Prompting

AI value multiplies when procurement collaborates with finance, sustainability, and operations.

**Examples**

Joint prompt with **Finance**: "Identify cost-to-serve per supplier and recommend payment-term adjustments."

Joint prompt with **Sustainability**: "Map top 50 suppliers by carbon footprint and propose decarbonization partnerships."

Joint prompt with **Operations**: "Optimise production schedule against supplier capacity and logistics lead times."

Such cross-functional prompting aligns AI outputs with enterprise goals.

## Ethical and Privacy Considerations

Prompting must respect confidentiality. Never include real supplier names, pricing, or contract details in consumer AI tools. Use anonymised data or approved enterprise platforms with privacy controls.

**Best Practice**

- Replace identifiers with codes (e.g., Supplier A, Supplier B).
- Disable model-training where possible.
- Store AI outputs within secure document systems.
- Responsible prompting builds both compliance and credibility.

**Sample Mini Case Study 19**

**Building Prompt Maturity in a Global Logistics Organization (Illustrative Case)**

*The following mini case is a fictional example designed to illustrate how structured prompt maturity enables scalable and reliable AI adoption in enterprise procurement and risk management. It does not describe a specific company or real-world program.*

A multinational logistics company introduced generative AI tools to 60 procurement professionals to support analysis, reporting, and supplier risk assessment. Early usage was informal and inconsistent, with individuals experimenting independently and generating uneven results.

To move beyond ad-hoc experimentation, leadership introduced a standardized prompting framework alongside a curated prompt library aligned to core procurement tasks. Training emphasized shared language, output expectations, and peer-reviewed prompt refinement.

As prompt maturity improved, average task completion time fell by 40%, and output quality became more consistent across the function. Within six months, the team produced an AI-generated quarterly supplier risk report that was adopted by the board as a regular decision-support artifact.

**Leadership Insight:** AI scales only when individual experimentation evolves into organizational capability. **Prompt maturity mirrors procurement maturity; the more structured the process, the more strategic the result.**

### Sample Prompts for Immediate Use

**Spend Optimisation**

"Analyse global spend data to detect duplicate suppliers and pricing anomalies. Suggest consolidation actions."

**Supplier Risk Dashboard**

"Create a 3-tier supplier-risk dashboard including financial, operational, and ESG metrics."

**Contract Clause Audit**

"Review ten supplier contracts for missing performance and sustainability clauses. Provide summary table."

**ESG Impact Summary**

"Generate a one-page ESG-impact summary for procurement's annual report, using tone suitable for investors."

**Negotiation Brief**

"Draft talking points for a supplier-review meeting aiming to balance cost savings with partnership continuity."

**Key Takeaways**

- Prompting is the new literacy of digital procurement.
- Structured frameworks yield consistent, executive-grade insights.
- Iteration and collaboration refine quality over time.
- Prompt libraries institutionalise best practice.
- Ethical discipline protects data and trust.
- A great prompt is like a great brief; clear, contextual, and confident.

# CHAPTER 6

## ADVANCED PROMPTING TECHNIQUES

Prompting is Both Art and Engineering.
At first, it wants to ask a search engine smarter question. But as your familiarity deepens, it becomes a design discipline; one that structures reasoning, simulates scenarios, and balances automation with ethics.

Advanced prompting allows AI to move from answering questions to **co-creating solutions**. In procurement, this means turning descriptive analysis into prescriptive strategy: not just what happened, but what should we do next and why?

This chapter introduces five advanced methods every AI-enabled procurement professional should master: **layered prompting, role-based prompting, scenario simulation, iterative refinement, and dashboard generation.**

Layered Prompting – Building Depth Step by Step
Complex procurement challenges are rarely solved in a single exchange. Layered prompting structures your interaction into logical phases; just as you would when running a sourcing project.

**Example: Supplier Evaluation**

**Prompt 1: Identify Candidates**

"List the top 20 regional suppliers of renewable-packaging materials based on reliability, ESG performance, and cost efficiency."

**Prompt 2: Evaluate Risks**

"For these 20 suppliers, rank potential operational and financial risks on a scale of 1–5."

**Prompt 3: Recommend Action**

"Select five suppliers for preferred-partner status and justify your selection in a 200-word executive summary."

Each layer feeds context into the next, mimicking professional due diligence.

It also reduces data overload, focusing AI stepwise as a human analyst would.

**Tip:** When handling sensitive data, use anonymised identifiers and store results in secure folders before applying any additional steps. If you have made mistakes in the past, stop now and ensure that all future sensitive data is properly anonymized.

Role Playing for Specialist Insight

AI responds differently depending on the perspective it adopts.

Assigning a role helps mirror expert reasoning and vocabulary.

Table 6.1: Role-Playing for Specialist Insight

| Role Type | Example Prompt | Expected Benefit |
|---|---|---|
| **Category Manager** | "You are a packaging category manager preparing a sourcing strategy for 2025." | Category-specific recommendations |
| **Risk Consultant** | "You are a supply-chain risk analyst assessing Tier-2 suppliers." | Prioritised risk matrix |
| **Negotiator** | "You are a senior negotiator engaging a supplier with rising prices." | Scenario-based conversation strategy |
| **Sustainability Auditor** | "You are an ESG auditor reviewing a supplier's carbon-reduction plan." | Policy-aligned improvement plan |

Professional roles prompt professional outputs, precise language, practical recommendations, and clearer logic chains.

**In prompting, perspective is performance.**

### Scenario Simulation – The 'What-If' Engine

AI excels at exploring alternative futures.

Scenario simulation helps procurement leaders stress-test plans before execution.

### Example – Raw-Material Price Surge

### Prompt A

"Simulate three sourcing scenarios if aluminum prices rise 20 % in Q2. Compare cost, lead-time, and supplier-risk impact."

## Prompt B

"Recommend mitigation actions balancing price stability and ESG commitments under each scenario."

**Output:** AI provides comparative tables and narrative assessments, effectively serving as a digital "war room."

### Benefits

Encourages anticipatory decision-making.

Provides quantitative and qualitative justification for board presentations.

Improves agility during crises.

### Real-World Use

A global automotive company ran AI-based simulations to model steel price fluctuations. When actual market shifts occurred, contingency plans were already board-approved, saving £14 million in unbudgeted costs.

## Iterative Refinement – The Continuous-Improvement Cycle

AI drafts quickly, but refinement converts quantity into quality.

### Process Overview

**Draft** – Get the first version quickly.

**Evaluate** – Review tone, accuracy, and feasibility.

**Re-Prompt** – Adjust parameters ("Increase ESG weighting to 40 %").

**Compare Versions** – Select best sections or merge insights.

**Finalize** – Convert into presentation-ready format.

Iteration mirrors the "Plan–Do–Check–Act" loop familiar in quality management. The aim is not to get it right once but to get it better every time.

**Sample Mini Case Study 20**

**Iterative Prompting for Responsible Supplier Evaluation in Pharmaceuticals (Illustrative Case)**

*The following mini case is a fictional example designed to illustrate how iterative prompting can improve the quality and governance alignment of AI-generated procurement artifacts. It does not describe a specific company or real-world deployment.*

A pharmaceutical company sought to improve the efficiency and consistency of its supplier evaluation process while maintaining alignment with responsible sourcing standards. The procurement team experimented with generative AI to design a standardized supplier evaluation form.

Rather than relying on a single prompt, the team adopted an iterative prompting approach, refining the output over five structured cycles. Each iteration adjusted scoring weights, clarified evaluation criteria, and improved alignment with ISO 20400 responsible procurement guidelines.

Through this process, the AI-generated form became clearer, more balanced, and easier to review. As a result, supplier evaluation review time fell by 30%, while evaluation accuracy and consistency improved by 25%, strengthening both efficiency and governance outcomes.

**Leadership Insight:** Quality emerges when AI outputs are treated as drafts to be refined, not answers to be accepted.

## Weighted Scoring and Prioritization

AI can apply weighted scoring models to balance multiple priorities.

This is essential when cost, risk, and sustainability must coexist in the same way.

### Prompt Example

"You are a procurement analyst. Rank 100 suppliers using a weighted scoring model: cost 40 %, delivery reliability 30 %, ESG compliance 30 %. Provide final scores and rationale."

### Why It Works

AI performs rapid calculations across data variables, producing prioritised                                                                                          results.
Human review ensures weight reflects organisational values.

### Sample Mini Case Study 21

### AI-Enabled Balanced Scorecard for Supplier Selection (Illustrative Case)

*The following mini case is a fictional example designed to illustrate how AI-driven scoring models can support balanced, values-based supplier selection. It does not describe a specific company or real-world procurement decision.*

A construction company sought to improve the rigor and transparency of its supplier selection process across a large subcontractor base. Historically, award decisions had been driven primarily by cost considerations, with sustainability and social factors applied inconsistently.

To address this, the company implemented an AI-enabled balanced scorecard to evaluate 80 subcontractors using weighted criteria. The model incorporated traditional cost and delivery metrics alongside ESG factors such as safety performance, environmental impact, and labor standards. Executives could adjust weightings to test different strategic priorities and see how rankings shifted.

While the lowest-cost suppliers initially ranked highest, the inclusion of ESG criteria significantly reshuffled the results. This broader view enabled leadership to make award decisions that better aligned with long-term risk management, reputation, and corporate values without sacrificing commercial discipline.

**Leadership Insight:** The smartest sourcing decisions emerge when leaders make trade-offs explicit rather than implicit.

## Dashboard and Report Generation

Well-designed prompts can instruct AI to generate dashboard layouts or written reports for internal communication.

**Prompt Example**

"Create a procurement dashboard template with KPIs for spend savings, supplier risk, ESG compliance, and cycle-time efficiency. Include data fields, visual chart suggestions, and refresh frequency." AI will typically be output:

- KPI list with formula logic.
- Suggested visual types (bar, line, heatmap).
- Recommended data sources.

These outputs accelerate collaboration with data teams and BI developers.

**Sample Mini Case Study 22**

**From Static Reporting to Real-Time Control in Logistics (Illustrative Case)**

*The following mini case is a fictional example designed to illustrate how AI-guided design can accelerate the shift from periodic reporting to real-time operational insight. It does not describe a specific company or real-world transformation.*

A logistics company sought to modernize its analytics approach, moving beyond static monthly reports that were slow to produce and quickly outdated. Leadership challenged the analytics team to reimagine how operational data could support faster, more informed decision-making.

To catalyze change, the organization used generative AI to define a structured dashboard design prompt, outlining required decision views, metrics, and user interactions. This prompt served as a blueprint for the analytics team, aligning business needs with technical execution.

Within one month, the team launched a live control tower integrating supplier performance, inventory levels, and freight movements into a single real-time view. As a result, monthly report preparation time dropped from five days to one, while leaders gained continuous visibility into operational performance.

**Leadership Insight:** Insight becomes transformative when leaders replace reporting cycles with decision-ready visibility.

Continuous-Learning Prompt Libraries
Teams that treat prompting as a collective craft evolve faster.

An **AI Prompt Library** becomes a living knowledge base, shared across procurement, finance, and sustainability functions.

## Library Maintenance Tips

- Version prompts by use-case (e.g., risk, spend, contracts). Record effectiveness notes.
- Review quarterly for updates to regulatory or ESG criteria.
- Over time, this repository becomes as essential as any procurement policy manual.

## Governance and Bias Mitigation

Advanced prompting carries greater influence, so governance becomes vital.

## Best Practices

- **Test for Bias:** Compare AI supplier rankings against human benchmarks.
- **Validate Data Sources:** Use approved, verifiable datasets.
- **Keep Human Oversight:** No final decision without review.
- **Audit Trails:** Log prompts, responses, and decision rationale.

These practices build defensible, ethical procurement operations. **Ethical AI is not slower, it's safer.**

## Sample Mini Case Study 23

## Scenario-Driven Negotiation Using AI Simulation (Illustrative Case)

*The following mini case is a fictional example designed to illustrate how AI-based scenario simulation can strengthen negotiation preparedness and outcomes. It does not describe a specific company or real-world negotiation.*

A European energy company faced a critical supplier negotiation with limited margin for error. To improve preparedness, the procurement team used generative AI to simulate potential supplier responses before entering discussions.

Using structured prompts, the model was asked to adopt different supplier personas risk-averse, cost-driven, and partnership-oriented and to respond accordingly to proposed negotiation positions. The procurement team rehearsed counterarguments and concession strategies against each scenario, identifying likely pressure points and areas for collaboration.

As a result, negotiators entered the discussions with greater confidence and clarity. The negotiation concluded with a 6% cost reduction and a more balanced long-term agreement, reflecting improved alignment between commercial terms and relationship objectives.

**Leadership Insight:** Preparation creates leverage when leaders use AI to test assumptions before they test positions.

Practical Prompt Templates for Advanced Users
**Scenario Modelling**

"Simulate three sourcing outcomes under different exchange-rate forecasts. Include sensitivity analysis."

## ESG Forecasting

"Predict supplier carbon-intensity trends over three years and suggest top five intervention levers."

## Crisis Management

"Generate a step-by-step contingency plan if a Tier-2 supplier in Asia halts production for two weeks."

## Spend Forecast Optimisation

"Model three procurement budget scenarios under 5 %, 10 %, and 15 % inflation."

## Stakeholder Report

"Prepare a 500-word executive summary explaining AI-derived risk insights in non-technical language."

## Key Takeaways

- Advanced prompting multiplies the value of basic AI tools.
- Layering and iteration produce structured, actionable intelligence.
- Role-based and scenario prompts convert analysis into foresight.
- Weighted scoring balances cost, risk, and ESG imperatives.
- Governance ensures fairness, transparency, and traceability.

**Prompting mastery transforms AI from an assistant into a strategic co-author.**

## CHAPTER 7

## GOVERNANCE, ETHICS & COMPLIANCE

Artificial intelligence can accelerate procurement performance but without governance, it can also amplify risk. Confidential supplier data, contract clauses, and spend analytics are highly sensitive. Every procurement professional therefore faces a dual responsibility: **to innovate and to protect.**

Governance is not bureaucracy; it is assurance. Ethics is not constraint; it is credibility. Together they create digital trust that allows AI to flourish safely within an organisation.

### Why Governance Matters

AI systems operate at scale and speed. A single flawed instruction or data breach can affect millions of pounds in spending and reputation. Governance ensures that decisions made by algorithms are traceable, fair, and aligned with policy.

Good governance asks three questions:

- **Is the data secure?**
- **Is the model fair?**
- **Is the decision accountable?**

If you can answer "yes" to all three, your organisation is practicing responsible AI.

### Data Privacy & Confidentiality
**Procurement's Data Sensitivity**

Supplier financials, pricing structures, and ESG disclosures are proprietary assets. Protecting them is non-negotiable.

Best Practice Safeguards

- **Anonymization:** Replace supplier identifiers with codes before analysis.
- **Access Control:** Restrict AI tools to licensed users only.
- **Encryption:** Ensure data is encrypted in transit and at rest.
- **Deletion & Retention Policies:** Allow users to delete AI interactions or export and clear them regularly.
- **Platform Governance:** Use enterprise versions such as ChatGPT Enterprise, Microsoft Copilot for 365, Google Gemini for Workspace, or Grammarly Business which guarantee that customer data is not used for public model training.

These measures turn AI use from a compliance risk into a competitive advantage built on trust.

**Sample Mini Case Study 24**

**Confidential Confidence in AI-Enabled Tender Evaluation (Illustrative Case)**

*The following mini case is a fictional example designed to illustrate how strong data governance and compliance practices can enable safe and effective use of generative AI in procurement. It does not describe a specific company or real-world deployment.*

A multinational logistics company introduced an enterprise-grade generative AI platform to support tender evaluation, aiming to accelerate analysis while improving consistency across bids. Given the sensitivity of supplier pricing and contractual data, leadership identified data security and confidentiality as critical prerequisites for adoption.

Before rollout, the Chief Procurement Officer required formal verification of encryption standards, access controls, and data-handling policies. In parallel, all users completed mandatory training focused on "no-share" principles, acceptable use, and escalation procedures for sensitive content.

With these safeguards in place, the platform was deployed across the tender evaluation process. The organization recorded zero data-breach incidents, while evaluation cycles shortened significantly due to faster document review and comparison. Compliance measures, rather than slowing adoption, became a foundation for confident and scalable use of AI.

Result: zero data-breach incidents and faster evaluation cycles. Compliance became an enabler, not a barrier.

**Leadership Insight:** Trust accelerates transformation when compliance is designed as an enabler, not an obstacle.

## Mitigating Bias & Ensuring Fairness

AI learns from data; if the data is biased, so are the outputs. Procurement leaders must audit algorithms for unintended discrimination, favoring large suppliers over SMEs, or certain regions over others.

**Bias-Reduction Strategies**

- **Diversify Data Sources:** Include suppliers from varied geographies and sizes.
- **Audit Outputs:** Compare AI risk scores with human assessments.
- **Weight ESG & Diversity Factors:** Balance cost and social value.

- **Document Decisions:** Keep an audit trail explaining final choices.

**Transparency converts doubt into discipline.**

**Sample Mini Case Study 25**

**Strengthening Supplier Diversity Through AI Fairness Controls (Illustrative Case)**

*The following mini case is a fictional example designed to illustrate how active bias mitigation improves fairness and outcomes in AI-supported procurement decisions. It does not describe a specific company or real-world initiative*

A global fast-moving consumer goods (FMCG) company deployed AI to support supplier evaluation and risk scoring across its procurement portfolio. Early results improved efficiency, but a review revealed that smaller and newer suppliers were consistently scoring lower due to limited historical data.

Recognizing the risk of unintended bias, procurement leaders initiated a model review. The AI was retrained using more balanced datasets that better represented suppliers of different sizes, regions, and maturity levels. In addition, manual review checkpoints were added for cases where data sparsity could distort automated scores.

Within one year, supplier diversity participation increased by 18%, while decision transparency and confidence improved across sourcing teams. The initiative reinforced the principle that fairness in AI systems requires deliberate design, not passive assumption.

**Leadership Insight:** Fairness does not emerge automatically from algorithms; it must be intentionally engineered.

## Regulatory Compliance Across Regions

Procurement now operates within a patchwork of laws:

Table 9: Regulatory Compliance Across Regions

| Region | Regulation | AI / Data Implication |
|---|---|---|
| EU | GDPR & Corporate Sustainability Reporting Directive (CSRD) | Data-handling and ESG reporting requirements |
| UK | Modern Slavery Act & UK Bribery Act | Supply-chain transparency and anti-corruption |
| US | FCPA & Dodd-Frank Act | Foreign-corrupt-practices and conflict-minerals disclosure |
| Africa | POPIA (SA) & local-content policies | Personal-data protection and domestic-sourcing |
| Asia-Pacific | PDPA (Singapore), China PIPL | Data-localisation and consent frameworks |

**AI tools must align with these regimes through configuration and oversight.**

**In Practice:** Integrate compliance checklists into AI workflows e.g., automatic alerts when supplier data touches restricted jurisdictions.

### Corporate AI Policies & Guidelines

A written **Responsible-AI Policy** anchors governance in daily behaviour.

## Core Elements

- **Purpose & Scope**: why the organisation uses AI.
- **Acceptable Use Rules**: approved tools, banned actions.
- **Human Oversight**: mandatory review points.
- **Data Security**: encryption, deletion, retention.
- **Ethical Principles**: fairness, transparency, accountability.
- **Audit & Reporting**: frequency and ownership.

## Sample Mini Case Study 26

## Governance by Design in Pharmaceutical AI Deployment (Illustrative Case)

*The following mini case is a fictional example designed to illustrate how embedded governance structures enable safe and scalable AI adoption in regulated industries. It does not describe a specific company or real-world rollout.*

A pharmaceutical company preparing for global AI deployment recognized that technology capability alone would not ensure compliance, trust, or sustainability. To address this, leadership established a formal AI Governance Board comprising representatives from Legal, IT, Procurement, Human Resources, and Compliance.

The board instituted quarterly reviews to assess model performance, data usage, ethical considerations, and regulatory alignment. Clear escalation paths were defined for potential issues, ensuring rapid response before risks could materialize during rollout across regions.

As a result, the organization achieved a smooth global deployment with no compliance breaches, while teams benefited from consistent guidance and decision clarity. Governance was embedded into operating rhythms rather than treated as after the fact control.

**Leadership Insight:** AI scales safely when governance is designed into the system, not layered on afterward.

### Ethical Use in Supplier Selection

AI-driven scoring must never override human ethics.

### Guidelines

- Validate algorithmic rankings before final awards.
- Publish selection criteria transparently.
- Include ESG weightings that reflect corporate values.

### Example
"An apparel retailer balanced AI's cost-efficiency recommendations with fair-labour commitments, awarding contracts to suppliers with verified ethical standards. The brand gained both savings and social credibility".

### Governance Framework for AI in Procurement

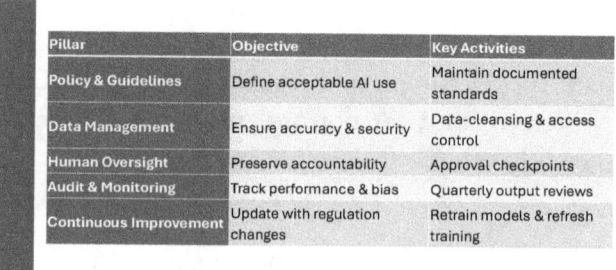

| Pillar | Objective | Key Activities |
|---|---|---|
| Policy & Guidelines | Define acceptable AI use | Maintain documented standards |
| Data Management | Ensure accuracy & security | Data-cleansing & access control |
| Human Oversight | Preserve accountability | Approval checkpoints |
| Audit & Monitoring | Track performance & bias | Quarterly output reviews |
| Continuous Improvement | Update with regulation changes | Retrain models & refresh training |

## Tools & Practices for Compliance & Ethics

- **Audit Logs**: record prompts and responses for traceability.
- **Bias-Detection Algorithms**: flag disproportionate scoring.
- **Supplier Screening Platforms**: verify sanctions & legal compliance.
- **Human-in-the-Loop Reviews**: require sign-off for high-risk outputs.

These tools embed assurance directly into digital workflows.

## Sample Mini Case Study 27

## Embedding Ethics in AI-Driven Global Supplier Risk Assessment (Illustrative Case)

*The following mini case is a fictional example designed to illustrate how ethical review and bias mitigation strengthen AI-supported supplier risk management. It does not describe a specific company or real-world deployment.*

A European fast-moving consumer-goods (FMCG) company deployed AI-driven analytics to assess risk across 200 global suppliers, integrating delivery performance, financial indicators, and compliance data. Initial results improved efficiency and visibility, but leadership initiated a post-implementation audit to test for unintended bias.

The audit revealed that the model disproportionately favored suppliers based in Western regions, driven by more complete historical datasets and reporting standards. To correct this, the organization introduced regional parity adjustments and increased the weighting of ESG and resilience factors within the risk model.

These changes improved fairness in supplier evaluation while also strengthening supply resilience by diversifying the network across regions. The revised model supported compliant, balanced sourcing decisions without sacrificing risk discipline.

**Leadership Insight:** Ethical AI does not weaken risk management; it makes it more robust.

## Cultural Foundations of Ethical AI

Ethics lives through people, not policies. Training programmes must cover:

- Data-privacy basics.
- Bias awareness.
- Scenario-based dilemmas ("Would we still approve this if AI hadn't suggested it?").
- Leaders should celebrate ethical decisions publicly, making integrity visible.

## Sample Prompt

"You are a procurement compliance officer. Create an AI governance checklist covering data privacy, bias mitigation, regulatory alignment, and human oversight. Present it as a table with ownership and review frequency."

## Key Takeaways

- Governance and ethics are enablers of innovation, not obstacles.
- Privacy, fairness, and accountability safeguard both data and reputation.

- Responsible platforms let users delete, export, and control their data.
- Continuous auditing builds long-term trust with stakeholders.
- A culture of integrity turns compliance into confidence.

**The most advanced algorithm is still guided by human conscience.**

# CHAPTER 8

## BUILDING AN AI-READY PROCUREMENT ORGANISATION

Artificial intelligence will not transform procurement by itself. The real transformation occurs when people, processes, and purposes align around a common digital vision. Becoming AI-ready is therefore less about installing new software and more about **preparing the organisation to think, learn, and decide differently**. This chapter outlines a practical roadmap for procurement leaders to embed AI confidently; covering readiness assessment, workforce training, change management, KPI design, and continuous improvement.

### Assessing AI Readiness

Before adopting AI, evaluate current maturity across four dimensions.

| Dimension | Guiding Question | Typical Symptoms of Low Readiness | First Actions |
|---|---|---|---|
| Data | Are data sets accurate and accessible? | Fragmented supplier records, inconsistent coding | Launch master-data-management clean-up |
| Process | Are workflows standardised? | Ad-hoc approvals, duplicate effort | Document and map key sourcing processes |
| Culture | Are teams open to digital tools? | Fear of replacement, silo mind-set | Run awareness sessions and showcase quick wins |
| Technology | Are systems interoperable? | ERP and SRM not connected, manual reporting | Integrate core platforms or deploy APIs |

**Readiness is not a pass-fail test; it is a mirror for progress.**

**Sample Mini Case Study 28**

**Data Readiness as a Catalyst for AI Success in Pharma Diagnostics (Illustrative Case)**

*The following mini case is a fictional example designed to illustrate the importance of data readiness in enabling effective AI adoption. It does not describe a specific company or real-world audit.*

A pharmaceutical diagnostics company initiated an AI readiness assessment to understand whether its data foundations could support advanced analytics and automation. The review revealed that approximately 40% of supplier data was stored in disconnected spreadsheets outside the organization's enterprise resource planning (ERP) system.

Recognizing this as a structural barrier, the company launched a data-cleansing and centralization initiative to standardize supplier records and consolidate them into a single, governed data environment. Ownership, access controls, and data quality standards were clearly defined as part of the effort.

Once data was centralized, subsequent AI pilot initiatives progressed significantly faster. Model development and testing cycles ran three times faster than earlier attempts, enabling teams to focus on insight generation rather than data remediation.

**Leadership Insight:** AI performance is ultimately limited by the quality and accessibility of the data beneath it.

**Workforce Training and Skills Development**

Technology adoption succeeds only when people feel capable and confident.

Four Core Skill Domains

- **AI Literacy**: understanding what AI can / cannot do.
- **Prompt Crafting**: writing structured, contextual instructions.
- **Data Interpretation**: reading dashboards and questioning anomalies.
- **Ethical Judgment**: recognizing when human review is essential.

**Upskilling is the new job security.**

**Training Ideas**

- 90-minute "AI 101 for Procurement" webinars.
- Peer-led prompt-engineering clinics.
- Simulation exercises using anonymised spend data.
- Ethics roundtables on privacy and bias.

**Sample Mini Case Study 29**

**Building AI Capability Through Targeted Workforce Enablement (Illustrative Case)**

*The following mini case is a fictional example designed to illustrate how targeted training programs accelerate AI adoption and improve workforce outcomes. It does not describe a specific company or real-world initiative.*

An electronics manufacturer introduced a tailored AI training program aimed at improving analytical productivity and confidence across its operations and procurement teams. While AI tools had been made available, leadership recognized that inconsistent skill levels limited their effective use.

The program focused on practical, role-specific use cases, standardized prompting techniques, and responsible AI guidelines. Employees were encouraged to apply new skills directly to everyday reporting and analysis tasks.

Within six months, average report-creation time fell by 30%, while employee satisfaction scores increased by 25%, reflecting both efficiency gains and improved engagement. The initiative demonstrated that workforce enablement is a critical enabler of sustainable AI value.

**Leadership Insight:** AI adoption succeeds when organizations invest as deliberately in people as they do in technology.

## Change Management and Adoption Strategy

Resistance is natural; clarity dissolves it. A structured approach based on **ADKAR** principles (**Awareness, Desire, Knowledge, Ability, Reinforcement**) keeps transformation human centered.

| Stage | Objective | Typical Activities |
| --- | --- | --- |
| Awareness | Explain why AI matters | Town-halls, leadership videos |
| Desire | Create personal relevance | Share "day-in-the-life" success stories |
| Knowledge | Teach how to use tools | Hands-on workshops |
| Ability | Practise new skills | Pilot projects with mentoring |
| Reinforcement | Sustain behaviours | Recognition and KPI alignment |

**People don't fear change; they fear confusion.**

97

## Integrating AI into Workflows

Embed AI where it amplifies, not complicates. Typical Integration Points

- Supplier onboarding: automated compliance checks
- Spend analysis: real-time dashboards.
- Contract review: clause extraction & expiry alerts.
- ESG tracking: auto-generated sustainability reports

**Sample Mini Case Study 30**

**Accelerating Supplier Onboarding with AI in Automotive Procurement (Illustrative Case)**

*The following mini case is a fictional example designed to illustrate how AI-enabled process integration can accelerate supplier onboarding while preserving human oversight. It does not describe a specific company or real-world implementation.*

An automotive group sought to reduce lengthy supplier onboarding cycles that delayed sourcing and innovation. Traditional approval processes involved multiple manual reviews across procurement, quality, and compliance functions, extending timelines without necessarily improving outcomes.

To address this, the organization integrated AI into the supplier onboarding workflow to automate document validation, flag missing information, and prioritize human review where risk indicators were present. Decision authority remained with procurement and compliance leaders throughout the process.

As a result, average supplier approval time fell from 21 days to 9 days, improving speed to value while maintaining governance standards. The initiative demonstrated that automation and oversight can coexist when roles and escalation paths are clearly defined.

**Leadership Insight:** Speed and control are not opposites when AI is designed to support not replace human decision making.

## Key Performance Indicators (KPIs)

Define KPIs that measure value and adoption, not just cost savings.

| Category | Example KPI | Target |
|---|---|---|
| Operational Efficiency | Time saved per sourcing cycle | > 25 % reduction |
| Data Quality | % of supplier data validated | > 95 % accuracy |
| Risk Management | # of disruptions avoided | Trend ↑ quarterly |
| Sustainability | % of suppliers with ESG scores | 100 % Tier-1 |
| Adoption Rate | % of team using AI tools weekly | > 80 % |

Link KPI reviews quarterly business updates to reinforce accountability.

## Continuous Improvement and Feedback Loops

AI evolves; so, your organisation must. Establish a rhythm of review and refinement.

- **Quarterly AI Review Board**: cross-functional meeting to assess results and risks.

- **Prompt Library Refresh**: update standard prompts with lessons learned.
- **Model Calibration**: retrain algorithms using new data sets.
- **Benchmarking**: compare maturity with peer organisations.

**Improvement is a culture, not a phase.**

**Sample Mini Case Study 31**

**Institutionalizing Learning Through Quarterly AI Reviews in Electronics Exporting (Illustrative Case)**

*The following mini case is a fictional example designed to illustrate how regular review cadences improve the effectiveness of AI-supported forecasting and risk management. It does not describe a specific company or real-world practice.*

An electronics exporter operating across multiple international markets introduced AI-based forecasting and supply-risk monitoring tools to support planning decisions. While initial results were promising, leadership recognized that model performance and assumptions needed regular validation as market conditions evolved.

To embed continuous learning, the organization established structured quarterly review sessions involving procurement, planning, and supply-chain leadership. These reviews examined forecast accuracy, emerging risk signals, and discrepancies between AI outputs and actual outcomes, enabling timely recalibration of models and decision thresholds.

As a result, forecast accuracy improved by 15%, and potential supply risks were identified two months earlier than under previous review cycles. The disciplined review process transformed AI from a static tool into a continuously improving decision asset.

**Leadership Insight:** AI delivers lasting value only when leaders treat learning as a cadence, not an event.

## Governance and Ethical Oversight

Strong governance, introduced in Chapter 7, must continue post-implementation. Appointing **AI Champions** in each category team.

- Conduct **Ethics Audits** every six months.
- Maintain **Prompt and Decision Logs** for traceability.
- Enforce **"Human in the Loop"** rules for high-risk decisions.

## Scaling AI Across Functions and Regions

Once pilots succeed, they expand carefully.

## Steps to Scale

- Standardize Prompts and Processes.
- Localize for Regulations and Language.
- Create Shared Centers of Excellence (CoE).
- Use Cloud Dashboards for Global Visibility.

## Sample Mini Case Study 32

## Scaling AI Value Across Categories in a Global FMCG Organization (Illustrative Case)

*The following mini case is a fictional example designed to illustrate how disciplined scaling amplifies both financial and sustainability outcomes from AI adoption. It does not describe a specific company or real-world rollout.*

Global fast-moving consumer goods (FMCG) company successfully piloted AI-enabled analytics within a single procurement category, delivering early cost and visibility gains. Rather than treating the pilot as an isolated success, leadership developed a structured scaling plan to extend the capability across additional categories.

Over time, the organization expanded AI adoption from one category to twelve, standardizing data models, governance controls, and performance metrics along the way. This disciplined approach ensured consistency while allowing category-specific customization.

As a result, the company achieved an additional 10% in cost savings beyond initial gains and improved ESG reporting quality by 20%, reflecting better data coverage, traceability, and confidence across the supplier base.

**Leadership Insight:** The real return on AI emerges when leaders scale what works without diluting discipline.

### Culture of Digital Curiosity

Encourage curiosity before compliance. Innovation flourishes when teams can ask, "What could AI do here?"

### Practical Ideas

- Monthly "AI Friday" knowledge-shares.
- Recognition for creative, ethical use cases.
- Internal storytelling around lessons learned.
- Culture eats technology for breakfast, curiosity feeds culture.

### Sample Prompt

"You are a procurement transformation consultant. Design a six-month roadmap to embed AI across supplier-management workflows, including training, KPIs, governance, and change-management milestones.

## Key Takeaways

- AI readiness requires balanced investment in data, people, and governance.
- Training builds confidence: confidence drives adoption.
- Integration works best where AI augments routine tasks.
- KPIs must measure learning as well as savings.
- Continuous improvement and ethical oversight sustain trust.

**AI success is not a project milestone; it is a mindset of perpetual learning.**

# CHAPTER 9

## FUTURE TRENDS IN AI-DRIVEN PROCUREMENT

The past decade turned data into a resource; the next will turn intelligence into infrastructure. Procurement is entering an age where machines not only inform decisions but participate in strategic design. To stay relevant, leaders must look beyond today's dashboards toward tomorrow's ecosystems; predictive, autonomous, and ethically intelligent. This chapter explores the emerging forces reshaping procurement and supply-chain management worldwide.

## Predictive and Prescriptive Analytics

### From hindsight to foresight

Predictive analytics uses historical and real-time data to forecast events such as price shifts or supplier defaults; prescriptive analytics recommends actions to optimise outcomes.

### Applications

- Forecast commodity price trends months ahead.
- Predict delivery-delay risk from weather or congestion data.
- Prescribe inventory or sourcing adjustments automatically.

### Sample Mini Case Study 33

### Predictive Foresight in Semiconductor Supply Management (Illustrative Case)

*The following mini case is a fictional example designed to illustrate how predictive analytics can provide early warning and strategic advantage in semiconductor supply chains. It does not describe a specific company or real-world event.*

A technology manufacturer operating in semiconductor-dependent markets deployed predictive analytics to monitor supply-demand dynamics, capacity signals, and upstream risk indicators. The objective was to anticipate shortages early enough to enable proactive sourcing decisions.

The models detected emerging patterns indicating a forthcoming chip shortage well before constraints became visible through traditional reporting. Armed with this foresight, procurement leaders secured production capacity and adjusted sourcing commitments ahead of market tightening.

These early actions avoided an estimated £8 million in potential production losses, while preserving customer commitments and operational stability.

**Leadership Insight:** Strategic advantage comes from seeing constraints before the market prices them in.

## Generative AI and Natural-Language Automation

Generative AI tools like ChatGPT Enterprise or Gemini move beyond analysis to creation: drafting contracts, RFPs, negotiation scripts, or ESG reports.

**Typical Use-Cases**

- Auto-draft RFPs include sustainability clauses.
- Generate supplier-performance summaries in executive tone.
- Create presentation decks directly from data.

Generative AI will evolve into autonomous co-authors, handling first drafts so humans can focus on refinement and judgment.

## Hyper-automation and End-to-End Orchestration

Hyper-automation combines AI, robotic process automation (RPA), and workflow management to link every step of the procurement cycle.

## Capabilities

- Auto-on-on-on-on-on-onboard suppliers using document recognition.
- Trigger approvals and payments through boots.
- Monitor compliance continuously.
- Automation removes friction; orchestration removes fragmentation.

## Sample Mini Case Study 34

## AI and RPA Integration in Pharmaceutical Procurement (Illustrative Case)

*The following mini case is a fictional example designed to illustrate how combining AI and robotic process automation (RPA) can transform transactional efficiency while strengthening compliance oversight. It does not describe a specific company or real-world implementation.*

A pharmaceutical group sought to modernize its procurement operations by reducing manual effort in purchase-order processing while improving compliance transparency. Legacy workflows required multiple handoffs and delayed visibility into approval status and exceptions.

To address these challenges, the organization integrated AI-driven document interpretation and exception handling with robotic process automation (RPA) for transaction execution. AI identified discrepancies and risk indicators, while RPA automated validated steps within the approval and posting process.

As a result, purchase-order processing time was reduced from three days to six hours, and compliance visibility improved through clearer audit trails and real-time exception monitoring. The initiative demonstrated how intelligent automation can deliver speed without compromising control.

**Leadership Insight**: Automation delivers its greatest value when intelligence and execution are designed to work together.

### AI-Enhanced Supplier Ecosystems

Future supplier networks will be dynamic and data rich. AI will score suppliers in real time on reliability, innovation, and ESG.

### Benefits

- Continuous qualification; no static vendor lists.
- Early identification of emerging partners.
- Shared predictive data for joint planning.

### Sample Mini Case Study 35: Automotive Innovation Network

An automotive OEM used AI to track supplier patents and R&D output, identifying innovative partners faster than competitors.

### Blockchain Integration

Blockchain adds immutable transparency to transactions; when combined with AI, it ensures data integrity and traceability.

## Examples

- Verify source of conflict-free minerals.
- Automate payments through smart contracts.
- Detect fraud through cross-validation.

### Sample Mini Case Study 36

### AI and Blockchain for Food Supply Integrity (Illustrative Case)

*The following mini case is a fictional example designed to illustrate how combining emerging technologies can strengthen product integrity and consumer trust. It does not describe a specific company or real-world deployment.*

A food manufacturer faced increasing pressure to protect brand integrity and ensure product authenticity across a complex, multi-tier supply chain. Traditional traceability systems provided visibility but were slow to detect manipulation or counterfeit substitution.

To address this, the company integrated blockchain-based traceability with AI-driven anomaly detection. Blockchain created an immutable record of product movement and provenance, while AI continuously monitored transaction patterns, volumes, and timing to identify irregularities indicative of counterfeit risk.

This combined approach enabled earlier detection and targeted intervention. As a result, counterfeit incidents were reduced by 30%, and transparency improvements strengthened consumer confidence in product authenticity and safety.

**Leadership Insight:** Trust is strengthened when transparency and intelligence reinforce each other.

## Sustainability and ESG Intelligence

Sustainability has become procurement license to operate. AI enables live measurement of carbon, labour, and governance metrics across multi-tier networks.

## Trends

- Predictive ESG analytics replacing manual audits.
- Supplier carbon benchmarking dashboards.
- AI supported circular-economy sourcing.

Tomorrow's procurement scorecards will measure emissions as closely as expenses.

## Predictive Risk Management

AI's ability to sense disruption will soon resemble a radar system; detecting weak signals from freight data, financial news, or social sentiment.

## Applications

- Geopolitical risk forecasting.
- Cyber risk detection via anomaly spotting.
- Early warning indices for supplier distress.

## Sample Mini Case Stuydy 37

## Proactive Resilience Through Predictive Logistics Intelligence (Illustrative Case)

*The following mini case is a fictional example designed to illustrate how predictive analytics can strengthen supply-chain resilience through early intervention. It does not describe a specific company or real-world incident.*

An electronics manufacturer operating global supply routes faced recurring exposure to port congestion and unplanned logistics delays. Traditional monitoring relied on carrier updates that often arrived too late to prevent downstream disruption.

To improve foresight, the company deployed predictive analytics using real-time port-sensor data, vessel traffic signals, and historical congestion patterns. The system flagged elevated delay risk well before shipments were impacted.

Armed with this early warning, logistics teams pre-booked alternative carriers and adjusted routing plans. These actions prevented an estimated £2 million backlog, preserving delivery commitments and stabilizing production schedules.

**Leadership Insight:** Resilience is achieved when leaders act on prediction, not reaction.

### Cognitive Procurement Assistants

Conversational AI will evolve into secure "co-pilots" embedded within ERP systems. Professionals will ask:

"Show me suppliers at ESG risk this quarter."

"Draft a renewal clause for the top-risk contract."

These assistants will combine generative AI with enterprise data, turning every buyer into a data-driven strategist.

## The Ethical Edge

As AI becomes ubiquitous, differentiation will come from responsibility. Firms that demonstrate transparent data-governance and fairness will attract both investors and talent. Expect third party "ethical AI certification" for suppliers within five years.

## Preparing for Emerging Technologies

Looking beyond 2030, several frontiers will reshape operations:

| Technology | Procurement Implication |
|---|---|
| Quantum Computing | Ultra-fast optimisation of complex supply-chain models. |
| Edge AI | Real-time analytics at warehouses and factories. |
| Digital Twins | Virtual replicas for scenario testing and sustainability impact. |
| Autonomous Procurement Agents | Systems executing micro-transactions within defined ethical boundaries. |

**The line between data, decision, and execution will blur; but ethics and governance must remain the anchor.**

## Key Takeaways

- Predictive and generative AI will redefine strategic agility.
- Hyper-automation will connect processes end to end.
- Blockchain and ESG analytics will institutionalise transparency.
- Cognitive assistants will personalize intelligence.

- Ethical stewardship will separate leaders from laggards.

**The future of procurement is not artificial; it is intelligently human.**

# CHAPTER 10

## THE HUMAN FUTURE OF PROCUREMENT

Every technological revolution eventually asks a moral question: What kind of humanity will we become because of it? In procurement, that question is urgent. The rise of artificial intelligence has brought efficiency and anxiety in equal measures. For some, AI feels like empowerment; for others, it feels like exposure. Yet history shows that every innovation, from the calculator to the cloud, first unsettled before it strengthened us. The future of procurement will not be defined by machines, but by **how responsibly humans use them**.

### Beyond Fear: Understanding the Real Risks

The loudest concern among professionals is clear: Will AI leak my data? The fear is valid. Procurement holds sensitive details supplier pricing, commercial terms, and confidential bids that no one wants outside the firewall. But many misconceptions persist about how enterprise-grade AI systems manage information.

**Reality**

Modern AI platforms designed for businesses apply **strict privacy-by-design principles**:

- **No training on your data:** ChatGPT Enterprise, Google Gemini for Workspace, Microsoft Copilot, and Grammarly Business all guarantee that user data is **not** used to train public models.

- **End-to-end encryption:** Data is protected both in transit and at rest.

- **User control:** You can **delete** chat histories, **export** data, or **disable** conversation retention entirely.
- **Independent security audits:** ISO 27001, SOC 2 Type II, GDPR compliance are now standard certifications.

**What Means for You**

You retain ownership of every idea, report, or analysis created within your corporate account. Fear fades when knowledge enters. Once professionals learn these safeguards, their posture shifts from avoidance to advantage.

## The Control Panel for Digital Trust

Trust is not blind faith it is informed choice. Most major AI tools now include built-in **control panels** for privacy and data management. Understanding them restores user confidence.

| Platform | Control Features | Notes for Procurement Use |
| --- | --- | --- |
| **ChatGPT Enterprise** | No data used for training; chat history can be disabled; admin analytics available | Use for internal strategy prompts and draft analysis; avoid public accounts for sensitive work |
| **Google Gemini for Workspace** | No-retention mode; enterprise data segregated by domain | Safe for summarising docs or generating RFP drafts |
| **Microsoft Copilot (for 365)** | Operates within corporate tenant boundaries; data never leaves Microsoft cloud | Ideal for Excel analysis and PowerPoint summarisation |
| **Grammarly Business** | No text stored or used for model training; GDPR compliant | Useful for refining contract language safely |

Knowing how to control your tools is the new cybersecurity.

Professionals who explore these settings rarely worry again; they simply build digital hygiene into their weekly routine.

### Ethics as the Next Competitive Advantage

As procurement becomes increasingly automated, **ethics becomes its signature of quality**. Stakeholders, investors, and consumers are now asking not just "How fast did you deliver?" but "How responsibly did you decide?"

Ethical procurement will soon define brand reputation as much as cost performance. AI offers data power; humans provide the moral compass.

### The Ethical Imperatives

- **Transparency:** Communicate how AI informs decisions.
- **Accountability:** Keep records of human review points.
- **Fairness:** Ensure smaller or emerging suppliers are not disadvantaged by algorithmic bias.
- **Purpose:** Align AI projects with organisational values, not just profit metrics. Technology amplifies intent; ethics determines direction.

### The AI-Ready Mindset

An AI ready professional is not necessarily technical they are teachable. They ask better questions, trust data without surrendering judgment, and welcome automation as an assistant, not a replacement.

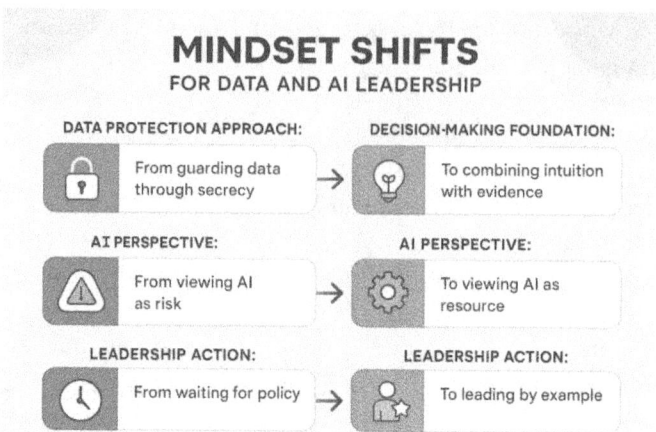

# MINDSET SHIFTS
## FOR DATA AND AI LEADERSHIP

**DATA PROTECTION APPROACH:**
From guarding data through secrecy → 

**DECISION-MAKING FOUNDATION:**
To combining intuition with evidence

**AI PERSPECTIVE:**
From viewing AI as risk →

**AI PERSPECTIVE:**
To viewing AI as resource

**LEADERSHIP ACTION:**
From waiting for policy →

**LEADERSHIP ACTION:**
To leading by example

**Sample Mini Case Study 38**

## Courage Through Clarity in Public-Sector AI Adoption (Illustrative Case)

*The following mini case is a fictional example designed to illustrate how transparency and education enable confident AI adoption in public-sector procurement. It does not describe a specific organization or real-world pilot.*

A public-sector procurement team in Africa was initially reluctant to pilot AI for tender review due to concerns about data privacy, misuse, and loss of control. These fears stalled experimentation despite mounting workload pressures.

To address this, leadership invested in targeted training focused on privacy settings, data-retention policies, and deletion controls. The team launched a tightly scoped pilot with clear boundaries on data use and escalation protocols.

Within weeks, tender processing time fell by 40%, while user confidence increased markedly. Team members reported a shift in mindset from apprehension to pride as understanding replaced uncertainty and enabled responsible experimentation.

**Leadership Insight:** Clarity creates courage when leaders replace fear of the unknown with informed control.

## Humanity in the Loop

Automation can calculate costs; it cannot measure consequences. Only humans can weigh trade-offs between short-term savings and long-term social value.

### Three Human Touchstones

- **Context:** Understanding the story behind the data.
- **Compassion:** Recognizing the people behind suppliers.
- **Conscience:** Asking not only is it "Can we?" but "Should we?"

The most advanced AI still requires moral interpretation. As one CPO remarked, "Our competitive edge isn't the algorithm it's our integrity."

### The Hybrid Workforce of the Future

The procurement function of the next decade will be hybrid by designing humans and AI systems working symbiotically.

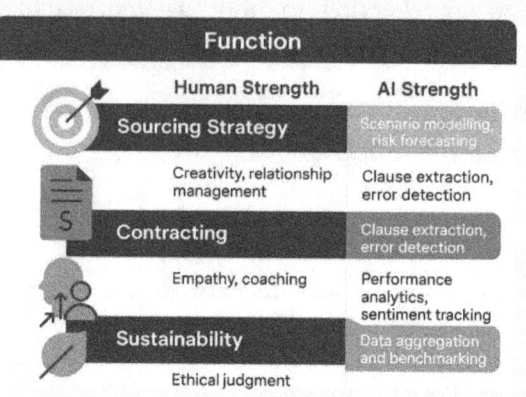

| Function | | |
| --- | --- | --- |
| | **Human Strength** | **AI Strength** |
| **Sourcing Strategy** | | Scenario modelling, risk forecasting |
| | Creativity, relationship management | Clause extraction, error detection |
| **Contracting** | | Clause extraction, error detection |
| | Empathy, coaching | Performance analytics, sentiment tracking |
| **Sustainability** | | Data aggregation and benchmarking |
| | Ethical judgment | |

Together they create a **cognitive partnership**: humans provide meaning; machines provide momentum.

## Culture and Leadership for the Human Future

To lead in this new era, procurement heads must champion both **competence and conscience**. They must show that trust and transparency are leadership behaviors, not compliance tasks.

## Leadership Practices

- Hold digital trust briefings quarterly.
- Reward teams for ethical use cases, not just savings.
- Include AI adoption in leadership performance metrics.
- Maintain open dialogue about privacy and ethics across departments.
- Great leaders translate fear into fluency.

## The 30-Day Adoption Sprint

A simple roadmap for teams ready to begin.

## 4-Week AI Adoption Timeline

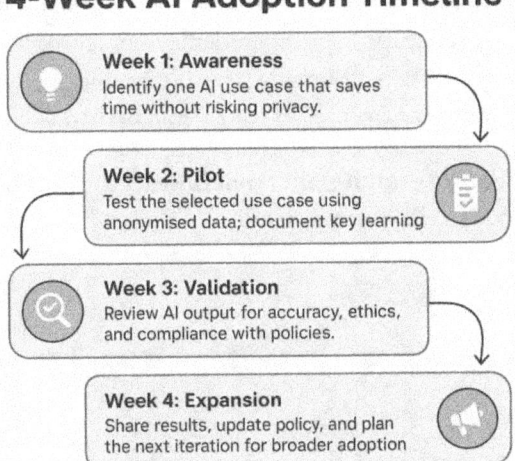

**Week 1: Awareness**
Identify one AI use case that saves time without risking privacy.

**Week 2: Pilot**
Test the selected use case using anonymised data; document key learning

**Week 3: Validation**
Review AI output for accuracy, ethics, and compliance with policies.

**Week 4: Expansion**
Share results, update policy, and plan the next iteration for broader adoption

**Start small, prove value, and scale responsibly.**

### The Global Mindset

Procurement is a global conversation about responsibility. Whether sourcing raw materials in Ghana, components in Malaysia, or services in London, the principle is the same: technology must serve humanity.

AI helps us collaborate across languages and time zones, but the heart of trade remains trust. The future procurement professional will be part data scientist, part diplomat, part ethicist.

### Reflection

AI is not here to replace human intelligence; it is here to remind us of its worth. The algorithms that now predict, summarise, and suggest cannot dream, empathize, or act morally. Those powers remain ours.

When fear of data leakage is replaced by understanding of **data control**, professionals rediscover confidence. When governance is seen not as red tape but as redemption, compliance becomes culture. And when humans lead machines with purpose, procurement moves from efficient to enlightened.

**"In the age of intelligent machines, the highest form of intelligence is still conscience."**

# CHAPTER 11

## THE AI-READINESS MATURITY MODEL & IMPLEMENTATION CANVAS

Every transformation needs a compass. For procurement leaders, that compass is the organization's ability to combine **technology, talent, trust, and transformation discipline.** The AI-Readiness Maturity Model provides a structured way to evaluate where you stand today and what must evolve to build a sustainable, human centered, AI enabled procurement function.

Think of this model as your **operating dashboard for digital maturity,** a living framework that evolves as technology, governance, and expectations advance.

### The Five Maturity Levels

| Level | Description | Typical Characteristics | Next Step |
|---|---|---|---|
| 1. Awareness | Initial exploration of AI possibilities | Sporadic experiments, no governance or data strategy | Build foundational literacy and appoint AI champions |
| 2. Experimentation | Early pilots and use-case testing | Small teams use open tools, uneven adoption | Define policy, choose secure enterprise platforms |
| 3. Integration | AI embedded in selected workflows | Standardised prompts, early KPIs, ethics oversight | Scale adoption and create prompt libraries |
| 4. Optimisation | AI linked across processes and regions | Dashboards, feedback loops, CoE in place | Refine models, formalise training and audits |
| 5. Transformation | AI as a strategic core capability | Data-driven culture, predictive analytics, trusted leadership | Innovate continuously, export best practice to partners |

Progress through the levels is cultural as much as technical.

The Four Capability Pillars

Each organization's readiness rests on four interconnected pillars:

| Pillar | Core Question | Measurement Focus |
| --- | --- | --- |
| People | Are our teams digitally literate and ethically confident? | Skills, adoption rate, cultural openness |
| Process | Are workflows structured for AI integration? | Standardisation, documentation, cycle-time reduction |
| Technology | Are systems secure, scalable, and interoperable? | Infrastructure, data integrity, analytics capability |
| Governance | Are we managing AI responsibly and transparently? | Policy maturity, audit trails, oversight frequency |

## The Four Capability Pillars for AI Readiness

| People | Process | Technology | Governance |
| --- | --- | --- | --- |
| Digital literacy and ethical confidence | AI-ready workflow structure | Secure, scalable, interoperable systems | Responsible and transparent AI management |
| Measured by skills, adoption rate, and cultuial openness | Focus on standardiseation, documentation, and cycle-time reduction | Assessed via infrastructure, data integrity analytics capability | Evaluated by policy maturity, audit trails, and oversight frequeny |
| • Digital literacy and ethical confidence | • Assessed via infrastructure | Evaluated by pulicy maturity | |

**Together, these pillars define the maturity baseline and reveal gaps between aspiration and reality.**

The AI Readiness Assessment Canvas

Leaders can complete this canvas quarterly or annually as a self-audit tool.

| Category | Current Status (1–5) | Target | Key Actions | Responsible Owner | Review Date |
|---|---|---|---|---|---|
| AI Strategy Alignment | | | Define AI objectives linked to corporate goals | CPO | |
| Data Quality & Access | | | Cleanse supplier data; integrate ERP & SRM | Head of Data | |
| Workforce Capability | | | Deliver AI-literacy and prompt-engineering training | HR / L&D | |
| Governance & Ethics | | | Implement Responsible-AI policy and quarterly audit | Compliance | |
| Technology Integration | | | Adopt enterprise-grade secure AI tools | CIO | |
| Change Management | | | Embed ADKAR-based engagement plan | Transformation Lead | |
| Measurement & KPIs | | | Track efficiency, savings, and ESG impacts | FP&A | |

The visual canvas (included in your appendix) acts as both a diagnostic and an action tracker.

## The Procurement AI Maturity Indicators

| Indicator | Early Stage (1-2) | Developing (3) | Advanced (4-5) |
|---|---|---|---|
| Prompt Use | Ad-hoc, inconsistent | Standardised templates | Enterprise prompt library maintained |
| Data Management | Siloed spreadsheets | Partial integration | Unified data lake with cleansing routines |
| Governance | Unclear ownership | Policy draft in progress | Active audits, bias monitoring |
| ESG Integration | Minimal tracking | Basic reporting | Automated ESG analytics integrated |
| Supplier Collaboration | Manual communication | Digital dashboards | Predictive collaboration using shared data |
| Decision-Making | Reactive | Data-supported | Predictive and prescriptive |
| Culture | Fear of automation | Learning mindset | AI-empowered innovation culture |

Use these indicators to score progress objectively and communicate maturity to stakeholders or auditors.

## Implementation Roadmap

A six-phase plan for rolling out AI across procurement:

| Phase | Focus | Key Milestones |
|---|---|---|
| 1. Vision & Sponsorship | Define purpose and appoint governance board | Executive mandate, AI policy draft |
| 2. Data Foundation | Cleanse and integrate data systems | 95 % supplier-data accuracy |
| 3. Pilot Projects | Test 2–3 use cases (e.g., spend analysis, supplier risk) | Lessons documented; ROI baseline |
| 4. Capability Building | Train all staff; establish prompt library | 80 % AI-tool usage rate |
| 5. Governance & Ethics | Activate audits and privacy controls | Quarterly reviews, zero breach record |
| 6. Scale & Innovate | Expand to multi-region operations | Global dashboards and CoE established |

Start small, scale ethically, learn continuously.

## Embedding Continuous Improvement

- **Quarterly Reviews:** Assess maturity shifts and reset targets.
- **Benchmarking:** Compare results within industry associations.
- **Feedback Loops:** Capture user suggestions to refine prompts and policies.
- **Recognition:** Reward teams who demonstrate ethical innovation.

Continuous improvement converts compliance into competitive advantage.

## Linking Maturity to Business Value

AI maturity must connect to tangible outcomes.

| Benefit Area | Early Impact | Mature Impact |
|---|---|---|
| Cost Efficiency | Basic spend visibility | Predictive sourcing savings |
| Risk Mitigation | Faster issue detection | Preventive risk elimination |
| ESG Compliance | Automated reporting | Real-time performance leadership |
| Talent Attraction | Digital curiosity | Global recognition as AI-ready employer |

## Linking Maturity to Business Value

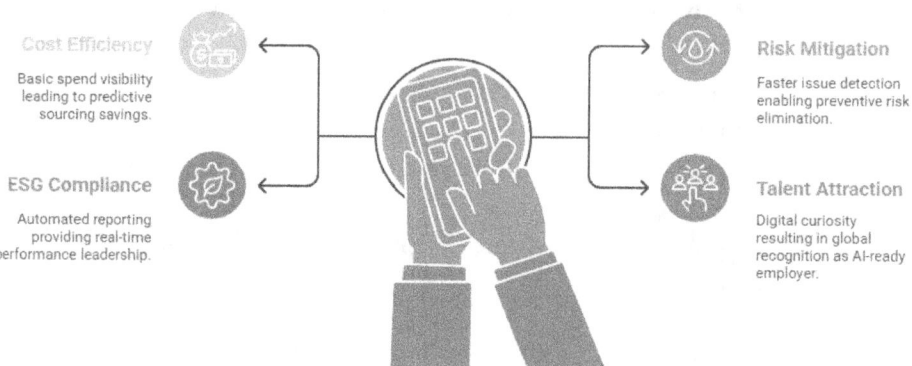

**Cost Efficiency**
Basic spend visibility leading to predictive sourcing savings.

**Risk Mitigation**
Faster issue detection enabling preventive risk elimination.

**ESG Compliance**
Automated reporting providing real-time performance leadership.

**Talent Attraction**
Digital curiosity resulting in global recognition as AI-ready employer.

Measuring these benefits ensures executive support and sustained funding.

### The Human Factor in Maturity

No model replaces leadership character. Empathy, integrity, and inclusion will determine how technology is used. The most advanced AI strategy still needs champions who model transparency, teach curiosity, and reinforce ethical courage.

Technology changes behaviour; leadership changes belief.

### Annual Maturity Review Prompt

"You are a procurement transformation officer. Conduct an annual AI readiness review using the five-level maturity model and four-pillar assessment. Summarise progress, highlight ethical-governance improvements, and recommend next-year priorities."

Including such prompts in management routines embeds reflection into strategy.

## Key Takeaways

- The AI-Readiness Maturity Model turns ambition into measurable progress.
- Balance investment across people, process, technology, and governance.
- Use Canvas to visualize priorities and assign accountability.
- Continuous review and ethical leadership keep maturity sustainable.
- True readiness does not reach Level 5; it is stay teachable at every level.
- Procurement's future belongs to organisations mature enough to innovate responsibly and humble enough to keep learning.

# CHAPTER 12

## AI AS YOUR DAILY CO-PILOT: REDEFINING THE PROCUREMENT PROFESSIONAL

### From System Readiness to Self-Readiness

In Chapter 11, we explored how organisations can measure and mature their readiness for AI. Yet transformation does not end with technology adoption or governance continues in the individual professional. Systems may be AI-ready, but are people self-ready? This chapter brings the conversation home—to the day-to-day life of procurement and supply-chain professionals. It reveals how AI can serve not only as a corporate tool but as a personal co-pilot: simplifying tasks, sharpening decisions, and amplifying human capability. The future of procurement will be built not by algorithms alone but by professionals who learn to partner with them—consciously, ethically, and creatively.

### The Everyday AI Toolkit

Artificial intelligence is no longer confined to analytics teams. Today, every buyer, analyst, and manager can work with a digital assistant that handles the repetitive so they can focus on the reflective.

**Inbox & Communication:** Summarise supplier emails, extract action points, and schedule follow-ups.

Example Prompt

"Summarise the last ten supplier updates and highlight overdue actions or risks."

**Meeting Preparation:** Draft agendas and talking points from performance data.

Example Prompt

"Create supplier-review talking points from last quarter's delivery metrics."

**Negotiation Support:** Simulate scenarios and counteroffers.

Example Prompt

"Generate three negotiation strategies to achieve 5 % savings while maintaining supplier goodwill."

**Document Creation:** Draft RFQs, RFPs, supplier-evaluation templates, and board summaries.

Example Prompt

"Produce an RFP template aligned with ISO 20400 sustainability guidelines."

**Research & Learning:** Summarise new regulations or ESG frameworks.

Example Prompt

"Explain the latest EU CSRD updates in under 200 words."

**Forecast & Spend Insight:** Translate dashboard data into narrative recommendations.

Example Prompt

"Interpret the current spend dashboard and list top three risk signals."

Every professional task becomes a conversation: ask, refine, validate, and act.

## The Strategic Co-Pilot

At managerial and leadership levels, AI evolves from assistant to strategic collaborator. It interprets complex datasets and converts them into foresight.

## Applications:

- Scenario Planning: "If freight costs rise 15 %, how does this affect our supplier mix and budget?"
- Real-Time Market Intelligence: Analyse sentiment and price movement before tender cycles.
- Executive Briefing: Convert technical dashboards into board-ready insights within minutes.
- Benchmarking: Compare supplier-diversity performance or ESG maturity against peers.

## Sample Mini Case Study 39

## Embedding Predictive Readiness in Global Manufacturing Procurement (Illustrative Case)

*The following mini case is a fictional example designed to illustrate how integrating AI-driven scenario modeling into routine planning enables rapid, confident response to market volatility. It does not describe a specific company or real-world event.*

A procurement director at a global consumer-electronics manufacturer embedded AI-based scenario models into the organization's monthly planning cadence. The models simulated the impact of commodity price movements, capacity constraints, and sourcing alternatives under different market conditions.

When aluminum prices spiked unexpectedly, the pre-built simulations immediately highlighted optimal sourcing adjustments and cost-mitigation options. Rather than convening a cross-functional taskforce, leaders reviewed scenarios and agreed on actions within minutes.

These rapid adjustments avoided an estimated £4.2 million in cost exposure. What previously required extended meetings became a five-minute, data-driven dialogue, demonstrating the operational value of predictive readiness.

**Leadership Insight:** Prepared scenarios turn volatility from a crisis into conversation.

## The Personal Development Partner

AI is not only a work enabler; it is also a mentor. Used intentionally, it becomes a personalized coach that accelerates professional growth.

**Practical Uses:**

- Create study plans for certifications such as CIPS, ISM, or sustainability modules.
- Draft LinkedIn thought-leadership posts and professional summaries responsibly.
- Simulate interview or negotiation practice through role-play prompts.

- Translate complex academic research into practitioner insights.

**Sample Prompt:**

"You are a professional mentor. Design a 4-week learning plan to build expertise in AI-driven risk analytics for procurement."

**Sample Mini Case Study 40**

**Learning in Motion Through AI-Enabled Micro-Learning (Illustrative Case)**

*The following mini case is a fictional example designed to illustrate how generative AI can support continuous professional development and capability transfer within procurement teams. It does not describe a specific individual or organization.*

A category manager in South Africa used generative AI to support preparation for CIPS Level 5 examinations. The tool generated weekly study questions, concise summaries of key sourcing principles, and simplified explanations of ISO 20400 responsible procurement concepts, allowing her to integrate learning into a demanding work schedule.

Beyond individual benefit, the manager adapted the approach for team development. She introduced AI-driven micro-learning prompts that delivered short, role-relevant learning modules during regular team interactions, reinforcing standards and shared understanding without formal training sessions.

This shift transformed learning from a one-off event into an ongoing practice. Individual certification success translated into broader departmental capability, demonstrating how AI can amplify learning when knowledge is deliberately shared.

**Leadership Insight:** Capability multiplies when learning moves from personal advantage to collective momentum.

### The Ethics and Empathy Compass

AI strengthens analysis; humans preserve empathy. The competitive edge lies in combining both. When systems rank suppliers purely on cost or data completeness, professionals must ask the ethical questions AI cannot:

- Is this supplier being penalized for lack of digital access?
- Does the lowest-cost recommendation align with our social-value commitments?

Embedding empathy keeps human procurement. Technology must serve equity, not efficiency alone.

*Guiding Principle: "AI reveals the numbers; professionals reveal the meaning."*

### The Daily AI Discipline Checklist

Adopt a short digital-ethics ritual each morning:

- Review Insights: Check overnight AI dashboards for spend, risk, and ESG alerts.
- Validate Outputs: Confirm critical decisions through human review (HITL).
- Document Learnings: Capture prompt successes and lessons in your team library.
- Secure Data: Clear chat histories or anonymised sensitive supplier details.

- Update Prompts: Refine your prompt templates weekly to reflect evolving needs.

Consistency creates confidence. Over time, these small habits convert novelty into normality.

## From Assistant to Advantage: The Career Horizon

AI is redefining what "value" means in procurement careers. Routine analysis is commoditized; interpretation, influence, and integrity are the new differentiators.

Emerging Roles:

- Decision Designer: Shapes how AI insights guide strategy.
- Data Translator: Bridges analytics and executive storytelling.
- Ethical Guardian: Ensures fairness, privacy, and inclusiveness in digital decisions.
- Prompt Architect: Builds and maintains prompt libraries as knowledge assets.

Professionals who master these hybrids skills will lead the next generation of Chief Procurement Officers.

## Sample Mini Case Study 41

## From Analyst to Strategist Through AI-Enabled Insight (Illustrative Case)

*The following mini case is a fictional example designed to illustrate how AI can elevate individual roles by shifting focus from data preparation to decision design. It does not describe a specific person or organization.*

A mid-level buyer at a logistics company began using AI tools to visualize complex supplier data and translate analytical outputs into concise narrative briefs. Previously, much of her time had been spent assembling reports and responding to ad-hoc data requests.

By automating data preparation and leveraging AI-assisted storytelling, she reframed supplier information around risk, opportunity, and strategic choice. Her dashboards emphasized implications rather than metrics, enabling senior leaders to engage directly with the underlying decisions.

Within six months, her analyses were being presented regularly at board-level meetings. Her role evolved not through formal promotion, but through a shift in how her contribution was perceived from data collector to decision designer.

**Leadership Insight:** AI creates strategic leaders by freeing people to focus on meaning, not mechanics.

The Human Multiplier

Procurement has always balanced numbers with nuance. AI amplifies the numbers; humans protect the nuance. When professionals blend digital precision with ethical judgment, they create outcomes faster, fairer, and more sustainable than either could achieve alone.

**"Machines calculate value; humans create it."**

AI as a daily co-pilot reminds us that intelligence is not just artificial it is augmented. The true transformation lies not in automation, but in the awakening of human potential through partnership.

## Sample Prompts

"Generate a daily procurement dashboard summary highlighting anomalies, savings, and ESG alerts."

- "Simulate three supplier-negotiation strategies that preserve relationship equity while reducing cost."
- "Draft a 300-word reflection on how AI is transforming procurement skills tone: professional LinkedIn post."
- "Design a 5-day micro-learning challenge for procurement teams to practise responsible prompting."
- "Translate supplier-performance data into an executive-ready one-page summary with key recommendations."

## Key Takeaways

- AI's greatest power lies in partnership augmenting daily work, not replacing it.
- Every procurement professional can use AI as a co-pilot for analysis, negotiation, and learning.
- Ethics and empathy remain the human differentiators in a data-driven world.
- Building daily AI discipline ensures responsible, repeatable success.
- The professionals who integrate technology into curiosity and conscience will define the future of intelligent procurement.

**"AI will not make you less human; it will make your humanity more visible."**

# CHAPTER 13

## THE INTELLIGENT HUMAN BRAND

### The Rise of the Intelligent Human Brand

The story of intelligent procurement does not end with automation or analytics it culminates in identity. After learning to collaborate with machines, professionals must now decide what defines them beyond efficiency. The age of data has rewarded precision; the age of intelligence will reward presence. The "Intelligent Human Brand" represents the evolution of professional credibility in a world where machines can replicate skill but never character. It is not a logo or profile, it is the visible integrity of a person whose decisions combine logic, empathy, and purpose.

In every boardroom, digital workspace, and negotiation table, professionals are being re-evaluated not only for what they can deliver but for how they lead amidst automation. The intelligent brand therefore emerges as a new currency; one measured by trust, not titles; by influence, not algorithms.

As procurement professionals become co-pilots with AI, their credibility shifts from technical mastery to relational intelligence. The market will remember not those who merely used technology but those who used it responsibly, creatively, and transparently.

### Character as Competitive Advantage

For centuries, skill defined employability. Now, character defines leadership. The Intelligent Human Brand is built on the premise that competence attracts attention, but character sustains influence.

In a digital economy saturated with knowledge, the differentiator is not data but discernment the ability to make ethical choices when no one is watching the dashboard. Integrity becomes a measurable KPI because it anchors trust between human and algorithm, client and supplier, leader and team.

Procurement, by its very nature, tests moral judgment daily: who to trust, what to disclose, which supplier practice to reward. AI multiplies those decisions, and with them, the moral load. A professional's character becomes the invisible algorithm behind every visible outcome.

**When integrity becomes habit, credibility becomes brand.**

**Sample Mini Case Study 42**

**Integrity as Influence in Renewable-Energy Procurement (Illustrative Case)**

*The following mini case is a fictional example designed to illustrate how ethical leadership decisions can protect enterprise value and shape industry influence. It does not describe a specific individual or organization.*

A global procurement director at a renewable-energy company faced pressure to accelerate supplier approval during a critical sourcing phase. She was offered a bonus-linked saving opportunity if she agreed to bypass a delayed ESG audit, allowing the project to proceed without full verification.

Despite commercial incentives, the director declined, insisting that sustainability claims must remain transparent, auditable, and defensible. She delayed final approval until the audit was completed, reinforcing governance standards across the sourcing process.

The audit subsequently uncovered a material mistake by a supplier that, if undiscovered, could have resulted in regulatory scrutiny and reputational harm. By holding firm, the organization avoided an estimated £3.6 million in penalties. The director's stance positioned her as a trusted ethics ambassador, both internally and across the wider industry.

**Leadership Insight:** Integrity becomes influence when leaders choose long-term trust over short-term gain.

## Digital Reputation and Thought Leadership

In an era where professional visibility often begins online, digital reputation is an extension of ethical behaviour. AI tools can amplify a voice, but only authenticity sustains it.

Procurement professionals once built credibility through years of project success; today, they build it daily through the ideas they share, the questions they ask, and the integrity of their online footprint. A well-curated digital presence is no vanity; it is public governance of one's professional intent.

AI can assist drafting posts, summarising insights, and analysing engagement. But the tone of humility, gratitude, and truth remains human territory.

Leaders should view platforms such as LinkedIn, professional forums, and CIPS communities not as stages but as classrooms: spaces to teach, learn, and contribute. Digital thought leadership is not about self-promotion but shared elevation the ability to translate personal learning into collective wisdom.

**Guiding Principle:**

"Use technology to project your values, not your vanity."

## The Human Branding Framework: The 4 Ps

To move from abstract inspiration to practical self-leadership, every professional can develop a personal brand through four dimensions Purpose, Proficiency, Presence, and Partnership.

### Purpose: Why Behind Work

Purpose clarifies identity. In a world of constant data noise, professionals with clear "why" stand out. Purpose is the bridge between capability and conviction.

### Ask: What outcome, beyond targets, do I want my work to achieve?

For procurement leaders, this might mean ensuring fair wages in the supply chain, championing sustainable sourcing, or mentoring young professionals. Purpose humanises metrics and turns results into legacy.

### Proficiency: Mastery in Motion

Proficiency is credibility earned through consistent performance. It reflects how confidently you navigate AI tools, interpret insights, and uphold governance. **AI does not replace expertise, it magnifies it**. The Intelligent Human Brand thrives when professionals combine digital literacy with sector knowledge, translating complexity into clarity for others.

Example: Using generative AI to create supplier-risk dashboards is technical skill; interpreting them in board language is proficiency.

### Presence: Visibility with Integrity

Presence is the art of being found for the right reasons. It encompasses digital footprint, professional communication, and interpersonal influence. Online, it means sharing knowledge responsibly and attributing sources. Offline, it means showing up prepared, respectful, and emotionally aware. **Presence is not noise; it is resonance the calm confidence that others associate with reliability.**

Tip: Before posting or presenting, ask, does this build trust or simply attract attention?

## Partnership: Collaboration as Signature

The most intelligent brands collaborate generously. They treat knowledge as a shared resource, not private property. Procurement leaders exemplify partnership when they co-create with suppliers, mentor peers, or contribute to cross-functional projects. Partnership multiplies influence and weaves ethical credibility into community reputation. When AI enables connection, partnership ensures compassion.

## Mini Global Cases Samples: Human Brands in Action

## Case 1: The Responsible Voice (UK | Illustrative Case)

*The following mini case is a fictional example designed to illustrate how individual leadership voice and ethical clarity can shape professional influence in the age of AI. It does not describe a specific person or organization.*

A category manager at a UK-based utilities company began sharing short weekly reflections on LinkedIn under the title "One Ethical Decision a Week." Each post described a real procurement dilemma such as supplier risk, sustainability trade-offs, or data transparency and how her team used AI dashboards to make decisions that were both commercially sound and ethically defensible.

141

Rather than promoting technology, the posts focused on judgment: what data was trusted, where human oversight was applied, and how transparency shaped outcomes. The clarity and consistency of her reflections resonated widely. Within months, her network expanded to include senior Chief Procurement Officers, regulators, and public-sector auditors.

As her visibility grew, she was invited to lead the organization's first Ethics-in-AI working group, helping formalize principles that others had previously treated informally. What began as a personal reflection practice evolved into a recognized leadership platform grounded in credibility and trust.

**Leadership Insight:** In the AI era, professional influence grows fastest when leaders are known for how they decide, not just what they deliver.

## Case 2: The Cross-Cultural Bridge (Singapore | Illustrative Case)

*The following mini case is a fictional example designed to illustrate how cultural intelligence and AI-enabled communication together can strengthen trust and resilience in global supply networks. It does not describe a specific individual or organization.*

A supply-chain professional based in Singapore managed supplier relationships across five countries, each operating in a different language and cultural context. To improve coordination, she introduced AI-powered translation tools into routine supplier communication, enabling faster information exchange without relying solely on intermediaries.

However, she treated translation as a starting point not a substitute for cultural understanding. Messages were reviewed and adapted to reflect local norms, tone, and expectations. Over time, suppliers reported feeling more respected and more willing to raise early concerns.

When severe flooding disrupted logistics in one region, the impact extended beyond schedules and contracts. The professional's established habit of multilingual, culturally sensitive communication allowed her to respond with empathy as well as efficiency. Suppliers prioritized transparency and collaboration, accelerating recovery in ways no automated workflow alone could have achieved.

Her ability to combine AI-enabled scale with human respect became a defining competitive advantage—strengthening relationships precisely when pressure was highest.

**Leadership Insight:** Technology may translate words, but trust is built when leaders translate with intent.

### Case 3: The Digital Steward (Kenya | Illustrative Case)

*The following mini case is a fictional example designed to illustrate how ethical technology stewardship and inclusive capability-building can expand value across procurement ecosystems. It does not describe a specific individual or organization.*

A young procurement analyst in Kenya recognized that many local small and medium-sized enterprises (SMEs) struggled to participate effectively in formal tenders—not due to lack of capability, but lack of access to tools and guidance. Rather than viewing these firms as marginal or competitive threats, he saw an opportunity to strengthen the regional supplier ecosystem.

Using freely available AI tools, the analyst began running informal training sessions for local SMEs, showing them how to prepare tender responses, structure documentation, and interpret evaluation criteria. The focus was not on gaming the system, but on readiness, clarity, and compliance.

By sharing skills instead of guarding knowledge, he helped raise the overall quality of supplier participation. Over time, several SMEs became reliable sourcing partners, improving competition, resilience, and diversity within the procurement network. His professional reputation grew—not through formal authority, but through trust earned by generosity.

What distinguished his impact was not technical expertise alone, but a stewardship mindset: using digital tools to lift others, not just optimizing outcomes.

**Leadership Insight:** Influence compounds when leaders use technology to expand opportunity, not just advantage.

### Using AI Responsibly to Build Your Brand

AI can now draft articles, generate professional summaries, and analyse engagement data. Used wisely, it accelerates communication; used carelessly, it dilutes authenticity. Responsible application involves three disciplines:

- Transparency: Disclose AI assistance in writing or publishing.
- Accuracy: Always validate facts and references manually.
- Voice: Edit for human tone replace perfection with personality.

Professionals who master this balance communicate faster yet sound truer.

**Sample Mini Case Study 43**

**Authentic Automation in ESG Communication (Illustrative Case)**

*The following mini case is a fictional example designed to illustrate how generative AI can amplify professional voice when authenticity is intentionally preserved. It does not describe a specific individual or real-world practice.*

A sustainability consultant began using generative AI to draft regular posts on ESG-related topics, enabling her to publish more consistently and cover complex themes efficiently. While the technology accelerated content creation, she was mindful of the risk that automation could dilute personal credibility.

To maintain authenticity, she adopted a simple discipline: every AI-assisted post ended with a short "human line" a reflection drawn from field experience, a moment of uncertainty, or a genuine question posed to peers. This final line signaled lived experience rather than polished abstraction.

Over time, reader engagement doubled. Feedback suggested that audiences could sense the difference between content that was merely generated and content that was grounded in real-world insight. The approach demonstrated that AI could scale communication without erasing the human voice that gives it meaning.

**Leadership Insight:** Automation amplifies impact only when leaders preserve the human signal within the noise.

## Sample Prompts

"You are a leadership-brand strategist. Draft a 200-word professional statement for a procurement leader known for ethical innovation in AI-driven sourcing."

"Analyse my LinkedIn profile summary for tone, credibility, and clarity. Suggest three edits to strengthen purpose and authenticity."

"Create a weekly content calendar for thought-leadership posts on responsible AI in procurement, including sample titles and focus themes."

"Write a reflective paragraph connecting sustainability goals with personal leadership values for inclusion in a professional bio."

Such prompts transform AI from a writing assistant into a mirror of self-awareness.

## The Future Currency of Leadership: Integrity, Innovation, and Influence

In tomorrow's digital economy, leadership credibility will be audited as rigorously as financial statements. The Intelligent Human Brand integrates three currencies that machines cannot counterfeit:

- Integrity: trust built through transparent choices.
- Innovation: creativity rooted in continuous learning.
- Influence: the capacity to move ideas ethically through networks.

AI may simulate style, but only humans can embody sincerity.

Procurement professionals who combine these currencies will lead not only projects but philosophies—showing that automation and altruism can coexist.

## Key Takeaways

- The Intelligent Human Brand is the evolution of credibility in the AI era.
- Character has replaced competence as the ultimate differentiator.
- Digital reputation must reflect authenticity and responsibility.
- The 4 Ps - Purpose, Proficiency, Presence, Partnership form a practical self-branding compass.
- Responsible AI amplifies ethical voices, not artificial ones. Influence grows when integrity becomes visible.

Technology may measure performance, but only humanity defines legacy. The most intelligent brand is not the one that commands algorithms but the one that inspires trust through conscience. In a marketplace where machines speak faster and data travel farther, leadership will belong to those who still listen, still care, and still mean what they say.

**In a world of intelligent machines, your humanity is your headline.**

## Epilogue: The Leadership Call

Artificial intelligence has handed procurement the greatest opportunity since globalization: the ability to make decisions that are faster, fairer, and more sustainable. But with that opportunity comes a responsibility that cannot be delegated to machines; the responsibility to decide with wisdom.

May every reader of this playbook lead with both intelligence and integrity, proving that technology is at its best when humanity is at its strongest.

## Selected References & Standards

The following sources informed the perspectives, frameworks, and themes explored in this book. They are provided for context and further reading and are not cited in relation to any specific case study.

McKinsey & Company. (2023). The state of AI in 2023: Generative AI's breakout year.

McKinsey & Company. (2025). Beyond automation: How generative AI is reshaping supply chains.

International Organization for Standardization (ISO). (2017). ISO 20400: Sustainable Procurement - Guidance.

Global Reporting Initiative (GRI). (n.d.). Global standards for sustainability impacts.

AIMultiple. (2023). AI procurement use cases and case studies.

## Glossary

AI: Artificial Intelligence; the simulation of human intelligence processes by machines.

Hyper-automation: The combination of AI, machine learning, and RPA to automate complex business processes.

ESG: Environmental, Social, and Governance criteria for evaluating a company's sustainability and ethical impact.

Prompt Engineering: Crafting inputs to AI systems to generate precise, actionable outputs.

Tier-2 Suppliers: Suppliers that provide goods or services to your direct suppliers.

www.ingramcontent.com/pod-product-compliance
Lightning Source LLC
Chambersburg PA
CBHW070936180526
45158CB00023B/1461